Vindicated

Vindicated

Closing the Hispanic Achievement Gap through English Immersion

By Johanna J. Haver

Foreword by Rosalie Pedalino Porter

ROWMAN & LITTLEFIELD
Lanham • Boulder • New York • London

Published by Rowman & Littlefield
An imprint of The Rowman & Littlefield Publishing Group, Inc.
4501 Forbes Boulevard, Suite 200, Lanham, Maryland 20706
www.rowman.com

Unit A, Whitacre Mews, 26-34 Stannary Street, London SE11 4AB

British Library Cataloguing in Publication Information Available

Library of Congress Cataloging-in-Publication Data

Names: Haver, Johanna J., author. | Porter, Rosalie Pedalino, 1931- author of foreword.
Title: Vindicated : closing the Hispanic achievement gap through English immersion / by Johanna J.
    Haver ; foreword by Rosalie Pedalino Porter.
Description: Lanham, MD : Rowman & Littlefield, [2018] | Includes bibliographical references and
    index.
Identifiers: LCCN 2018022451 (print) | LCCN 2018047217 (ebook) | ISBN 9781475841145 (elec-
    tronic) | ISBN 9781475841121 (cloth : alk. paper) | ISBN 9781475841138 (pbk. : alk. paper)
Subjects: LCSH: Language policy--United States. | English-only movement--United States. | English
    language--Political aspects--United States. | Education and state--United States. | Education,
    Bilingual--Political aspects--United States. | Education, Bilingual--Government policy--United
    States. | Education, Bilingual--Law and legislation--United States. | Immersion method (Lan-
    guage teaching)
Classification: LCC P119.32.U6 (ebook) | LCC P119.32.U6 H388 2018 (print) | DDC 306.44/973--
    dc23
LC record available at https://lccn.loc.gov/2018022451

This book is dedicated to Lloyd,
my loving husband and partner in life's adventures.

Contents

Foreword

English for the Children, a campaign that changed laws and education policy in three states, is one of the most successful citizen-led initiatives in recent history.

Immigrant children have always been at a disadvantage during the brief transition period when they do not understand the language or the lessons taught in the classroom. I was one of these children, sitting in a first grade classroom in Newark, New Jersey, understanding not a word. Richard Rodriguez wrote movingly of just such an experience in his autobiographical *Hunger of Memories*. Little or no special help was given to such children, who were expected to "pick up" the language and learn something—or eventually leave school for unskilled work.

Enter the brilliant experimental theory introduced at the height of the civil rights years—the notion that non-English-speaking children deserve special help to learn English, to enable them to learn their school subjects, and avail themselves of equal educational opportunities. The program proposed to meet this need was called *bilingual education* and it required all school subjects to be taught in the native language of the child for most of the school day, with an added English language lesson. The expected benefits of this program included learning math, science, reading, writing, in a language already native to the child; not falling behind in these subjects; and increased self-esteem from having one's home language validated in the classroom, which would lead to greater academic success. After a period of three years, students would move from learning in their native language to a full mastery of the English language for regular classroom work.

As a newly minted Spanish/English bilingual teacher at the start of this experiment, I was a true believer. A year or two of classroom teaching forced me to understand the truly egregious failings in the theory. In practical terms, the problems were obvious: Teaching Latino children in Spanish most of the school day did nothing to develop their English language skills, and segregating these students from all but brief contact with their English-speaking classmates did not increase anyone's self-esteem. Local and state education authorities were slow to document the academic performance of students in bilingual programs, but eventually the truth began to seep through all the feel-good advance predictions.

After twenty years of bilingual education research, Rossell and Baker in their 1996 report *The Emperor Has No Clothes* gave us the true metaphor. The program was counterintuitive and damaging to the children it was intended to help. Students remained in substantially separate bilingual classrooms beyond the original three-year limit, often up to five or six years, without mastering the language skills they needed to succeed in regular classroom work. These failings were reluctantly admitted in California, the state enrolling the highest number of non-English-speaking students; in Arizona, the state with the highest proportion of Spanish-speaking children in its school demographics; and in Massachusetts, where the state determined there were no measurable benefits for native language instruction. But each year, when we activists testified before state committees in favor of changing policy, the response was to do nothing, nada, zip.

In the well-researched account that follows, Johanna Haver provides the essential information about the English for the Children campaign in California that resulted in a 61 percent favorable vote in 1998 to drop bilingual education and give students structured English immersion programs instead. Arizona followed in 2000 with a similar referendum campaign that won 63 percent of the vote in that heavily Latino state on the Mexican border. My home commonwealth of Massachusetts, the most ideologically liberal place in the known universe, turned out a 68 percent favorable vote. How could this happen?

One must credit the genius, work ethic, and sustained commitment of Silicon Valley software guru Ron Unz. What a credit to the American way: He saw a devastatingly bad situation and dedicated his time, energy, and resources to fix it. Unz did the heavy lifting to give the English for the Children campaign high visibility. He bankrolled the signature gathering to get the referenda on state ballots. He enlisted and inspired leaders in each of the three states to write, speak out, and put our energies into the cause. He is a master at public relations.

Haver meticulously describes how the changes came about that revolutionized the teaching of students who temporarily lack facility in the English language. How to teach young children a new language is hardly rocket science, requiring a new method to be created from scratch. The Greeks and Romans, probably the Hittites and Egyptians, handed down lore about their efforts in this area. The essentials are well known even if they had to be rediscovered by some of my colleagues: Start as early as possible (age five being ideal); hire teachers knowledgeable about the ways of teaching listening comprehension, speaking, reading, and writing skills in the new language; give the students a substantial number of hours of instruction; allow students to move as rapidly as their individual abilities dictate; and provide opportunities for learning and recreational activities with native speakers of the target language. Most students, given these intensive learning opportunities from the first day of school, will master the new language well enough to learn school subjects taught in that language in an average of one to two years.

Substantial data is reported in these chapters attesting to the successful outcomes in all three states. Hard data on the academic achievement of formerly non–English speakers show measurable progress. Our students in English immersion programs learn the language rapidly to a level sufficient for inclusion in regular classrooms. In time, many of these students outperform their native English-speaking classmates on state tests of reading and math, as is well substantiated in California and Massachusetts.

A personal aside: I cannot omit a success story occasioned by my consulting for a group of local educators and parents who started a Chinese immersion charter school that uses the principles of structured immersion language teaching. The school is such a phenomenal success that its students, while learning in Mandarin up to half the school day, also score at a high level on state tests of reading and math in English. Pioneer Valley Chinese Immersion Charter School is the only K–12 Chinese immersion school in the United States. The basic elements for its success: competent teachers, a well-designed curriculum, and a longer school day to accomplish the learning of both the second language and the school subjects.

Does any logical person argue with success? Why would any group of people ignore the proven progress made by our newest schoolchildren thanks to the educational opportunities they have received—opportunities never available to earlier generations of immigrant children? Sorry to say, it has indeed happened. Perhaps a generation of success has bred complacency. New efforts have been undertaken by legislators and "community leaders" in California and Massachusetts, and in 2017 a new education law was enacted in Massachusetts and a referendum question passed in California—both of which weaken the English-teaching model, opening the door again to those old bilingual programs. It is as if we have learned nothing from experience. Curses! Foiled again.

The public has been sold a new bill of goods: the promise of bilingual programs to help our *English-speaking* children become bilingual, leading to a blossoming of high school graduates fluent and literate in two languages. Hurrah for the idea—but can such a large-scale goal be met? For starters, it would require a longer school day (certain to be opposed by teachers' unions) along with cadres of special teachers fluent and literate in two languages (not easy to find). But the most deplorable part of this misleading idea is that it is not focused on the needs of the 5 million non-English-speaking children presently making up the fastest-growing segment of our school-aged demographic.

We who have advocated for these children over the past few decades express one hope: that educators in California and Massachusetts move slowly in dismantling the successful English immersion programs and that legislators in those two states leave this arena to the educators, without putting their unwieldy thumbs on the scales by pouring new money into the old sour-vintage bilingual receptacles. My second sincere hope is that Arizona continues in its role as a beacon to the other states for the excellence of its teaching of immigrant children.

Haver's text is of prime importance to teachers, administrators, policy makers, parents, and all people of goodwill who value the achievable goal of giving our newest students the skills to become active participants in the classroom and the larger community of our nation.

Rosalie P. Porter, EdD
Singer Island, Florida

Preface

On November 2, 2002, the people of Massachusetts voted overwhelmingly to rescind the thirty-one-year-old law that mandated the teaching of bilingual education, originally called *native language instruction*, to children whose primary language was other than English. Instead, the limited-English students would learn English through sheltered English immersion techniques.

With backing from scholars of national repute and gubernatorial candidate Mitt Romney, the Massachusetts English Language Education in Public Schools Initiative (Question 2) passed by a whopping margin of 68 versus 32 percent of the vote. The turnout and support from residents in urban Latino districts in the Boston area were especially impressive. Massachusetts had become the third state—after California in 1998 and Arizona in 2000—to derail bilingual education.

After celebrating his win that night, Silicon Valley software entrepreneur Ron Unz, the originator and leader of the English for the Children movement, stepped away from his mission to bring an end to an instructional program that had proven ineffective. He had spent nearly seven years of his life and in excess of $2 million of his own money on this venture.

That same night, Phoenix attorney Tom Horne was also celebrating at his Arizona home after winning his bid for Arizona state superintendent of public instruction. Like Unz, Horne was committed to ending bilingual education. As a man who spoke three languages fluently, Horne was well aware that immersion in a new language for several hours every day is a requirement for mastery.

Soon after being sworn in, Horne began the process of implementing Arizona's English for the Children initiative, which had passed two years earlier but had not gone into effect due to political interference from the bilingual education establishment.

This book is a second edition to *English for the Children* in that it retells the story of Ron Unz's and Tom Horne's political battles both during and after their campaigns. It provides updates on the policies and progress of the English learner programs in the four states that either voted for or against the English for the Children ballot measures as well as New York City's English language learner (ELL) programs, where Unz attempted but failed to create a citizens' initiative.

It is important to not confuse the preferred bilingual education programs for limited-English students, dual-language and transitional bilingual education, with what is offered at long-established dual-language schools. Parents send their children to these schools to learn all their subjects in both English and a second language through immersion techniques. These parents are almost always professional people who are themselves proficient in English and are able to support their children with language learning at home. The Amigos School in Cambridge, Massachusetts, and Davis Bilingual Magnet School in Tucson, Arizona, are examples of such schools. The principals and teachers there must maintain high standards in order to cover their two-language curricula. If a student cannot keep up or is disruptive, that student must leave.

In dual-language schools for limited-English students, a small group of English-dominant students shares instruction with a much larger group of usually Spanish-dominant students, with the purpose of both groups becoming bilingual in both languages. From the early grades, most of the instruction is in Spanish. Thus the English-dominant students have a good shot at gaining fluency in their second language, whereas it is highly unlikely that the Spanish-speaking students will master their second language, English. It is important to note that these programs are funded by federal and state dollars meant for limited-English students to become English proficient—not for English-proficient students to learn Spanish or any other language.

With transitional bilingual education (TBE), the process is similar to that of dual language—minus the presence of English-dominant students. The Spanish speakers receive their instruction in a segregated setting with other Spanish-dominant students. Typically, in preschool and kindergarten, they are taught in English for only 10 to 20 percent of their instructional time, which equals from twenty-two to forty-four minutes per day in a half-day setting. In first grade, they receive about 30 percent of their full-day instruction in English; in second grade, 35 percent; in third grade, 50 percent; and in fourth and fifth grades, 60 percent.

Both dual language and TBE for limited-English students contradict what linguists consider basic to second language learning: Children learn a second language best and most easily if immersed in that language at an early age, ideally from four to six years old, for several hours daily. Thus Spanish-speaking students in these bilingual classes are unlikely to achieve English proficiency unless they are immersed intensively in English outside of school for two to four additional hours. That is a highly unlikely scenario for immigrant children from Spanish-speaking communities, whose parents usually speak little English and can barely afford to pay for basic needs, much less English tutors.

Having taught Hispanic limited-English students from impoverished neighborhoods for nineteen years, I disagree with bilingual education because of both my own experiences and the evidence that has shown it to be ineffective. Moreover, in the past few years, structured (or sheltered) English immersion has proven more successful than anyone could have anticipated in the three states in which it was mandated. The limited-English students in California, Arizona, and Massachusetts have become proficient in English at a young age and are doing well in mainstream classes. Like other students, many of them have been able to attend college and pursue meaningful careers.

As the title implies, *Vindicated* makes the case that Ron Unz had it right all along.

Acknowledgments

I decided to write this book after receiving new information regarding the *Flores* class action lawsuit, which had not been resolved at the time of my former book's publication. Eric Bistrow, lead attorney for the state of Arizona, provided me with a chapter from his memoirs that reveals the unrelenting perseverance that culminated in a decision at the US Supreme Court and, from there, a final conclusion. Tim Hogan of Arizona Law in the Public Interest, the attorney who represented the plaintiffs, sent me transcripts of courtroom testimonies that brought to life in a personal way this compelling story.

Sandra Stotsky, former senior associate commissioner at the Massachusetts Department of Elementary and Secondary Education, offered suggestions and provided me with firsthand knowledge. I admire her steadfastness to help others to improve education in their states, as she was able to do brilliantly in Massachusetts.

Crucial to this book was the in-depth research completed on bilingual education as it applies to English language learners by professors Joseph Guzman of Michigan State University, Charles L. Glenn of Boston University, Christine Rossell of Boston University, and Marie T. Mora of the University of Texas, as well as Dr. Mark Hugo Lopez of the Pew Research Center. They showed courage in challenging bilingual education orthodoxy.

Rosalie Pedalino Porter helped me by editing and critiquing my entire manuscript. Her assistance was invaluable. I cannot thank her enough.

I am grateful to editor Tom Koerner for his encouragement and his assistant Carlie Wall for always being available to answer my questions.

Introduction

Cracks in the Foundation

Bilingual education has changed considerably since the passage of the Bilingual Education Act in 1968. This law, known also as Title VII, is an amendment to the Elementary and Secondary Education Act (ESEA) of 1965. It provides school districts with federal funds to support special programs for children who do not have sufficient command of English to do regular classroom work in that language.

Initially, the law did not require these children to be taught in their native language. However, as our society focused increasingly on the civil rights of minorities, the federal government encouraged some degree of instruction in the home language for limited English proficient (LEP) students, mostly speakers of Spanish. This was never a federal mandate.

Separate classes for LEP children, apart from English speakers for part of the school day, was intended to be a temporary arrangement. Three years was deemed an adequate amount of time for LEP students to learn enough English to function academically in mainstream classes. Gradually the time of participation extended to as many as seven years and sometimes even longer, with an unacceptably high number of Hispanic students either dropping out of school or graduating without having learned English beyond a basic level.

It was not until the early 1970s that *bilingual education* became synonymous with *native language instruction.* US senators Edward Kennedy and Walter Mondale initiated a bill that required schools receiving federal grants to provide instruction in the children's native language and culture. Whereas the bill was expected to pass easily in the Senate, it was not popular in the House. Representative Herman Badillo, a strong supporter of the bill, lobbied his colleagues relentlessly but to no avail.

Badillo's staff then discovered an old, little-known rule that allowed legislation to pass with a yes/no vote in only one house of Congress, as long as it was considered but not rejected in the other house. Thus Badillo read a carefully prepared script that made it possible for him to say he had introduced the bill on the House floor and then again when it came up for debate. Both times Badillo withdrew the bill before it could be voted on.[1]

The Senate approved the bill and the House/Senate conference committee adopted the measure as an amendment to the Bilingual Education Act, which was incorporated into the total ESEA of 1974. The new native language instruction requirement was applied specifically to 96 percent of grant funding and thus became a monetary incentive for what we now call bilingual education.

While lobbying for the bill, Badillo had often suggested that his colleagues fly down to Florida to see for themselves what he considered an impressive dual-language program.[2]

DADE COUNTY DUAL-LANGUAGE PROGRAM

In the 1960s about a million refugees, mostly middle class and well educated, fled Fidel Castro's Communist revolution in Cuba and settled in Dade County, Florida. Their intent was to return to their homeland after Castro was overturned, so it was understandable that they wanted their children to retain and further develop their proficiency in Spanish.

Beginning in 1961, a group of mostly exiled professors from the University of Havana implemented a dual-language program at a Dade County elementary school. The students received their lessons in Spanish for half of the day and in English during the other half. In subsequent years, the program was extended to additional schools.

The conclusion of a 1966 school district report stated that the pupils were rapidly becoming "culturally advantaged" in that they were learning to operate effectively in two languages and two cultures.[3] However, twenty-one years later, the Dade County Public Schools' *Evaluation of the Bilingual Curriculum Project* of 1987 found there to have been no advantage in teaching school subjects to limited-English students in their native language.[4]

At the time, Badillo insisted that "the quality of instructors was so high and the motivation of the parents and students to retain their Spanish was so strong that anyone who visited their classrooms left impressed."[5]

Three decades later Badillo expressed regret regarding the implementation of the amendment he had helped pass into law: "The reality of what has occurred since 1974 has been a complete distortion of the bilingual-education law."[6] As a citizen of Hispanic heritage, he stated in an open letter, "We are proud of our heritage and our culture, but to keep children in classes where their own native language is used in the hope that they will somehow make the transition to English after five or six years is unacceptable to us."[7]

LAU V. NICHOLS

In 1970, San Francisco activist lawyer Edward Steinman filed a class action suit on behalf of Kinney Lau and 1,789 other Chinese students who were failing in school because of their inability to understand and speak English. Steinman won his case when the Supreme Court ruled in 1974 in *Lau v. Nichols* that schoolchildren who do not know English must be provided with special assistance to remove the language barrier to an equal education.

Soon thereafter, some school districts were found to be negligent in implementing the *Lau* decision. For that reason, US Commissioner of Education Terrel Bell introduced the *Lau* remedies in 1975. These guidelines told districts how to identify and evaluate children with limited English, what instruction to use, when children could be considered ready for mainstream classrooms, and what professional training should be provided for teachers. The remedies set time limits and were used for negotiating consent agreements. They were never approved by the US Congress.

When elementary schools were found to be out of compliance with the *Lau* remedies, federal government officials directed them to provide bilingual education—that is, native language instruction—and English as a second language (ESL) lessons. Intensive English language instruction was considered sufficient in secondary schools. School districts had no choice but to comply or face losing federal funding.[8]

In 1981, a month after President Ronald Reagan's inauguration, Bell—newly appointed as secretary of education—rescinded the *Lau* remedies that he had issued six years earlier. Bell now called the guidelines "harsh, inflexible, burdensome, unworkable, and incredibly costly."[9]

AMERICAN INSTITUTES FOR RESEARCH STUDY

In 1977, the American Institutes for Research (AIR) reported on a study of Spanish/English bilingual programs encompassing 286 classrooms that had been in operation for at least four years. The LEP students in these bilingual programs not only scored more poorly on tests of English but also scored no higher in mathematics than comparable LEP students who were not enrolled in bilingual education.[10]

Critics of bilingual education pointed to the study as proof of its ineffectiveness. Bilingual education advocates blamed the poor results on data gained from a later study indicating that 49.6 percent of the teachers in those projects were not proficient in their students' mother tongue.[11]

Undoubtedly, a shortage of truly bilingual teachers continues to be a problem in teaching children in two languages on a large scale. Most people who consider themselves to be bilingual favor one language, with limited conversational and literacy ability in an additional one. Maintaining oral and academic proficiency in two or more languages is a challenging feat that requires years of study and continual perseverance.

MOMENTUM CONTINUES

In 1971 Massachusetts became the first state to pass a transitional bilingual education act mandating the implementation of bilingual education in every public school where twenty or more LEP students of the same language background were enrolled.[12] The state's strict provisions became a model for similar laws that passed in California in 1972, Texas in 1973, and New Jersey in 1974.

Advocacy for bilingual and bicultural education increased during the late 1970s and early 1980s, promoted by the theories of college of education professors Jim Cummins of the University of Toronto and Stephen Krashen of the University of Southern California. Both of these professors insist to this day that multiculturalism and instruction in the native language are essential to the academic achievement of LEP students, however much research has proven otherwise.

Teacher candidates interested in second language instruction have been required to read and master the views of Cummins and Krashen in most colleges of education in the United States. For this reason, many new teachers begin their careers enthused about bilingual education. Until legislative changes were made starting in the late 1990s, they learned little or nothing about immersion techniques that are based on a carefully formulated approach of teaching English to LEP students as soon as they enter school.

CULTURAL DEMOCRACY

In 1978 Alfredo Castaneda, P. Leslie Herold, and Manuel Ramirez III, three noted professors of education, coined the phrase *cultural democracy*, which they identified as a new philosophy for Mexican-American children.[13] They believed that American public education had failed culturally diverse children by not providing them with their language and their heritage as part of their school experience:

> The fundamental message to the child whose home and community socialization experiences have been different has been, "Learn our ways and forget about your own." To do so, however, implies betrayal of home and community

as well as forsaking everything that is familiar and comfortable. Not to switch loyalties is to risk nearly unmanageable conflicts at school. [14]

A movement was afoot that encouraged the development of the first language: Spanish, in most cases. Starting in the 1980s, Massachusetts imposed the requirement on all schools to include lessons on each LEP student's history and culture as part of the curriculum. This became an especially difficult rule to follow due to the growing number of districts with one or two dozen different languages present in the LEP population.

SÖDERTÄLJE PROGRAM IN SWEDEN

To justify bilingual education, Cummins often wrote and talked about the success of the Sodertalje program in Sweden, where Finnish students learned first using their native language as their major language and then continued with Finnish and Swedish through elementary school. He said this resulted in the Finnish children reaching almost the same academic level as the Swedish children by the sixth grade. [15]

Charles Glenn of the Boston University College of Education was the state official responsible for the Massachusetts bilingual education law, so he was particularly pleased to learn of the Swedish program's success. However, while visiting Sweden in the mid-1990s, Glenn became dismayed after talking with experts in the field and reading a great deal of Swedish research. He found that Cummins had seriously misrepresented the Swedish program.

Glenn was provided with an assessment by Swedish-American linguistics researcher Christina Bratt Paulston, who concluded, in a report commissioned by the Swedish government, that the so-called mother-tongue classes existed strictly because of Finnish national demands and that the outcome had been disappointing. According to Swedish education researcher Lars Ekstrand, the proportion of the Finnish immigrant pupils who required extra help in Swedish had grown from 41 percent in 1975 to 69 percent in 1983 as a result of the Finnish program. [16]

THOMAS AND COLLIER STUDY

Cummins, Krashen, and other college of education professors have often cited the studies by Wayne Thomas and Virginia Collier of George Mason University as proof of the effectiveness of bilingual education. The researchers analyzed and compared the achievement scores of LEP students over a six-year period, beginning in 1981, in Fairfax, Virginia.

The LEP students who had already learned to read in their native languages before immigrating showed higher achievement over several years than the ones educated solely through ESL in Fairfax. The researchers believed that students who had learned certain subjects in their native language first had an academic advantage over the other students.

They broadened their investigation to encompass the long-term achievement of language-minority students in five large school districts in various areas of the United States. In 1995 Thomas and Collier concluded, "It is very clear from all of our findings in this study, as well as other researchers' work, that when students have the opportunity to do academic work through the medium of their first language, they are academically more successful in the long term in their second language."[17]

Like the results reported concerning the Sodertalje program in Sweden, the Thomas and Collier study supported Cummins's "threshold hypothesis" that literacy and other skills transfer to a second tongue only after a minimum level of cognitive-academic language proficiency has been achieved in the native language. However, also like the Sodertalje program, serious problems were found with the Thomas and Collier study. Christine Rossell, professor of political science at Boston University, put forth the in-depth analysis "Mystery on the Bilingual Express: A Critique of the Thomas and Collier Study" in 1998. Among the many problems she identified, some stood out as particularly egregious:

- It is not a true longitudinal study that covers eleven grades, as claimed; each grade consists of different students.
- Results were discarded, without explanation, because the researchers considered them "ungeneralizable." That no details of the omissions are offered makes replication of this study impossible.
- Lengthy and fallacious criticisms of the scientific method are made as justification for not using proper research methods. The likelihood that only the top Hispanic students in bilingual programs are compared to most of the students enrolled in immersion programs gives bilingual education an unfair advantage.
- The average test scores for English learners in the two-way bilingual programs of the study are from 20 to 22 percentile points higher in grades five through eight than those of three well-regarded two-way bilingual programs in actual school districts. This suggests that the test scores of native speakers have been included with those of LEP students, and thus the results cannot be considered valid.[18]

Rossell concluded that the study's unscientific methodology could have produced misleading results and that its lack of data set "a new low in federal grant reporting."[19]

THE NATIONAL RESEARCH STUDY

The National Research Council (NRC) study of 1997 was the work of a committee of twelve research scholars led by Stanford University College of Education professor Kenji Hakuta and Dr. Diane August of the council staff. The two-year study was funded by the US Department of Education and many private foundations. The purpose was to examine the research that had accumulated during the twenty-nine prior years concerning how limited-English students were taught, and to make recommendations.

Charles Glenn wrote a review of the study. Rosalie Pedalino Porter, director of the Institute for Research in English Acquisition and Development (READ), summarized Glenn's main points:

- There is no evidence of long-term advantages or disadvantages to teaching English learners in their native language.
- Teaching children to read in English first, rather than their native language, has had no negative effects.
- Emphasizing cultural and ethnic differences has been counterproductive in that it has led to stereotyping and reinforcement of the differences between English language learners and native speakers. It does not lead to better self-esteem.
- Research does not support the idea that teachers who are themselves members of minority groups are more effective than others who work with children from those same groups.
- The US Department of Education's management of bilingual education research has been a total failure—wasting hundreds of millions of dollars [specifically for the research] and using the research agenda for political purposes to justify a program of questionable worth [bilingual education].[20]

EFFECTS OF BILINGUAL EDUCATION IN THE LABOR MARKET

In 1998 READ published "The Labor Market Effects of Bilingual Education among Hispanic Workers" by Mark Hugo Lopez, director of Hispanic research at the Pew Research Center, and Marie T. Mora, professor of economics at the University of Texas. At the time Lopez was an assistant professor at the University of Maryland with a PhD in economics from Princeton University; Mora was an assistant professor at New Mexico State University with a PhD in economics from Texas A&M University.

They analyzed "High School and Beyond," a 1980 study of the national longitudinal data collected by the National Center for Education Statistics (NCES). It included more than fifty thousand high school sophomores and seniors, with language program data collected on more than eleven thousand base-year participants. The survey provided information on wages and occupations for ten years past high school, with clear indicators of whether students participated in ESL or bilingual education programs.

Lopez and Mora concluded that Hispanic immigrants who had gone through bilingual education programs ended up earning considerably less than those who had learned English exclusively through ESL methods: "While there are other potential explanations for the differences we observe, at a national level, our results suggest that bilingual education programs as they are currently implemented may widen the socioeconomic gap between LEP students and English proficient populations over time."[21]

In 2002 the quarterly journal *Education Next* published "Learning English," by Joseph M. Guzman, economics professor and director of the Chicano and Latino Studies Program at Michigan State University. He holds a PhD in business and master's degrees in business research, economics, and statistics from Stanford University.

Guzman evaluated the same NCES longitudinal data as Lopez and Mora and agreed with their conclusions on wages. He reached additional results regarding the education of limited-English Hispanic students:

- The best performance of Hispanic English learners was found among students from Spanish-speaking households who had made a rapid transition to English, either through ESL programs or through English immersion.
- The outcomes were considerably worse for students who had switched from one program to the other, due to the inconsistency and disruptive effects of being exposed to two diametrically opposed methods of language acquisition.
- The clear indication was that any positive returns owing to bilingual instruction were outweighed by the associated costs of delaying transition to English. By not attending to deficiencies in English by the critical age of five or six, catching up became problematic.
- The mixed results in the literature could be due to confusing the beneficial effects of growing up in a bilingual household with the negative influences of bilingual instruction. In other words, maintaining Spanish at home while learning English as well and as quickly as possible at school presented the best possible outcome.[22]

DISSATISFACTION GREW

Educators, politicians, and Hispanic activists supported bilingual education as the best way for children to learn English, despite the lack of valid, reliable evidence. Nonetheless, due to its poor results, bilingual education began losing popularity among the public as early as the late 1970s.

The provision of the ESEA that required most federal grant funds to be spent in support of native language instruction programs continued until 1984, when it was reduced from 96 to 75 percent of the total federal allotment. At last, a modest amount of federal money began to be invested in English immersion programs.

As the low achievement of Hispanic LEP students became a serious concern, bilingual education advocates insisted privately that the fault lay with the children, frequently the offspring of farmworkers, who they believed did not have the capability to do well in school. Those advocates continued to state in public forums the decades-old discredited notion that LEP children need to be taught in their native language in order to develop self-esteem and appreciation for their heritage.

Educators and parents rarely spoke up, even if they had doubts whether learning mostly in Spanish would promote proficiency in English. Most of them either accepted the bilingual education explanations or kept quiet because they feared being accused of either racism or insensitivity to the merits of bilingualism.

Some government officials—such as California superintendent of public instruction Delaine Eastin and Governor William Weld of Massachusetts—recognized the situation and tried to do something about it, but failed. The published research of Christine M. Rossell and books by Rosalie Pedalino Porter and Linda Chavez gave wide visibility to the issue. Nevertheless, no one could figure out a way to do something constructive about what was increasingly proving to be a terrible injustice committed against children with limited proficiency in English.

Finally, in 1996, Silicon Valley software entrepreneur Ron Unz let the world know that it was time to end bilingual education for LEP students. That year he began English for the Children, a movement that continues to this day to have a positive impact on LEP children in the three states where the voters have approved Unz's ballot measures.

Chapter One

Running the California Political Gauntlet

A sequence of events occurred in California in the mid-1990s that caused a political shift that exists to this day. Since 1996, California Democrats have been able to build and maintain their lead over the Republicans in the state assembly, state senate, US House of Representatives, and US Senate. Political science experts have attributed this development to a surge in the turnout of Latino voters at the polls.

The trend began in 1994, after California became the first state in the country to pass legislation related to immigration with Proposition 187, a ballot referendum known as Save Our State (SOS). This measure banned the estimated 1.3 million undocumented residents in California from receiving health care, public education, and other social services, and it penalized anyone who failed to enforce its provisions.

Governor Pete Wilson, a Republican, and several Republican legislators campaigned vigorously for the referendum because they believed the state could no longer afford to pay for the social services of so many people in the state illegally. Their opponents insisted that the law was discriminatory against Latino and Asian immigrants.

The initiative passed with nearly 59 percent of the vote. An exit poll on Election Day showed that 78 percent of Republicans and 62 percent of independents favored it, while 64 percent of Democrats opposed it. However, it was never enforced because it was found in federal court to be unconstitutional.

Two years later, in November 1996, another issue of concern to Latinos appeared on the ballot: Proposition 209, known as the California Civil Rights Initiative, an anti–affirmative action measure led by Republican University of California regent Ward Connerly that prohibited any state institution from considering race, sex, or ethnicity in the areas of public employment, public contracting, or public education. Already unhappy with the Republicans for approving Prop 187, Latinos registered en masse and voted as Democrats at the polls against Prop 209.

The Latinos' vote was not strong enough to defeat Prop 209; it passed with 54 percent of the vote. However, their vote added Democrats to Congress and gave them control of the state assembly. Thus began the decline of the Republican Party's clout in California.

AWARENESS OF BILINGUAL EDUCATION'S FAILINGS

During this politically turbulent time, a wave of dissatisfaction with bilingual education arose among Californians. For nearly thirty years the state had sustained the most rigorous bilingual programs in the country, but they were not working. Of the approximately 1.3 million children identified as limited English proficient in 1995, approximately 79 percent were Spanish speakers and were required to participate in the bilingual programs. The cost per annum specifically for educating language-minority children amounted to $300 to $400 million, with only sixty thousand students (5 percent) reaching English proficiency each year.

In 1995 California Superintendent of Public Instruction Delaine Eastin and the State Board of Education considered many proposals to loosen the bilingual education restrictions. Eastin stated, "We have to be honest enough with one another to say, when something isn't working, it's time to re-examine it. There has to be a point at which we bite the bullet and say, 'At least they have to learn English.'"[1]

In other parts of the country, similar awareness was growing. Linda Chavez, a conservative nationally syndicated columnist, wrote frequently about the inadequacies of native-language instruction, another term for "bilingual education." In *Out of the Barrio*, Chavez calls for political changes that would lead to Hispanic assimilation.[2] In 1995 she founded the Center for Equal Opportunity (CEO) to provide legal support to parents in New Mexico who opposed bilingual education in their state. CEO later expanded to include several services related to race and ethnicity.

Rosalie Pedalino Porter's book *Forked Tongue* tells about the author's personal experiences with the politics and failures of bilingual education.[3] Porter is featured in chapter 5 of this book as an expert witness in the *Flores* lawsuit and in chapter 9 as a leader of the English for the Children of Massachusetts movement.

Boston University professor Christine Rossell, with social science researcher Keith Baker, put forth the book *Bilingual Education in Massachusetts: The Emperor Has No Clothes*, a thoroughly-researched work that exposes the pitfalls of native language instruction as a means of teaching English to language-minority children.[4] Rossell is mentioned throughout this book as an expert researcher in the area of bilingual and immersion education. She was also a leader of the Massachusetts movement.

California education officials urged the federal authorities to allow California school districts more say regarding their programs. Yet Eugene Garcia, director of bilingual education and minority languages affairs at the US Department of Education, demurred. In Garcia's opinion, local control of the program could result in immigrant children's language needs being ignored. He explained, "I've seen this before and kids will be hurt by this climate, directly and indirectly."[5]

Republican Massachusetts governor William Weld had proposed a three-year limit on bilingual education, but the state's legislature rejected it in 1995 (see chap. 9, pp. 112–13). Other state legislatures were considering similar measures at the time but passed nothing of significance. In other words, an increasing number of people had become aware of the problem but were unable or unwilling to do anything about it.

THE BIRTH OF ENGLISH FOR THE CHILDREN

The movement to dismantle bilingual education actually began on February 14, 1996, when financial software developer Ron Unz picked up the *Los Angeles Times* and read an article article titled "80 Students Stay Out of School in Latino Boycott." Latino parents had boycotted Ninth Street School, located in downtown Los Angeles, because their children were not learning English.

Alice Callaghan, an Episcopal priest who was running Las Familias del Pueblo, a community program for some of the school's students, led the boycott. At onetime a supporter of bilingual education, Callaghan stated later that she did not care if it worked in theory, because it did not work in practice. To make her point to reporters, she distributed copies of a completed homework assignment from a sixth grader that read, "I my parens permi in dis shool en I so I feol essayrin too old in the shool my border o reri can grier das mony putni gire and I sisairin aliro sceer."[6]

Soon thereafter Unz established and became chairman of the English for the Children movement in California. Highly successful with his software company, he had the time and the money necessary to organize and fund a movement that would ultimately derail bilingual education in three states and curtail the funding of it at the federal level.

Influential Latino Californians tried to dissuade Unz from going forward with his movement. Linda Chavez, the most famous foe of bilingual education in the country, warned him against creating another proposition so close on the heels of propositions 187 and 209. She feared it could worsen California's racially charged political climate. Pointing to the Ninth Street School protest, Unz assured Chavez and other doubters that Latino parents would be his most ardent supporters.[7]

Unz found people to join his cause who were used to taking hits for criticizing bilingual education. They would know what to expect. Rossell, whose research had debunked bilingual education, helped Unz write the initiative that would give citizens the opportunity to vote on the issue. Gloria Matta Tuchman, an admired California Hispanic educator who had been advocating immersion techniques for years, became cochair of the movement and cosponsor of the initiative.

The famous math teacher Jaime Escalante, whose experiences teaching calculus to Hispanic children are chronicled in Jay Mathews's book *The Best Teacher in America*[8] and the movie *Stand and Deliver*, was named honorary chairman. Fernando Vega, a respected Hispanic political figure in the San Francisco area, was given the same title.

Unz provided extensive information about the progress of his initiative through e-mails and on his website English for the Children.[9] His followers were kept abreast of daily happenings at a time when people were first becoming accustomed to the internet. At his website, he invited people to contribute personal narratives, which were mostly bilingual education horror stories. Unz's website remains a great source of information regarding the initiatives.

THE FIRST UNZ INITIATIVE

The Unz initiative for California stated that all children "shall be taught English by being taught in English and all children shall be placed in English language classrooms." Furthermore, "children who are English learners shall be educated through sheltered English immersion during a temporary transition period not normally intended to exceed one year." Waivers were allowed for "children who already know English," "older children" (age ten or older), and "children with special needs."[10]

Starting with the year the initiative was enacted, a sum of $50 million was allocated every year for ten years for adult English language instruction to "parents or other members of the community who pledge to provide personal English language tutoring" to LEP children. Moreover, parents or legal guardians were granted "legal standing to sue for enforcement of the provisions of this statute," and "any school board member or other elected official or administrator who willfully and repeatedly refuses to implement the terms . . . may be held personally liable."[11]

SUPPORT AND OPPOSITION

Unz had credibility among the California Latino population because of his strong, vocal opposition to Prop 187 and for national identity cards, an issue associated with that initiative. He was well known in that state because of his challenge to Governor Pete Wilson in the 1994 Republican primary when, at the age of thirty-four, he had drawn 34 percent of the vote away from the incumbent. Anyone with less impressive credentials and less money to invest in the English for the Children movement would likely have been defeated because of the powerful entities determined to maintain bilingual education programs.

Unz's initiative was opposed by a number of groups, including the Mexican American Legal Defense and Educational Fund (MALDEF), the California Association for Bilingual Education (CABE), the American Civil Liberties Union (ACLU), the California Latino Civil Rights Network, the Educational Alliance for the California School Boards Association, the California Association of School Administrators, both teachers' unions (the California Federation of Teachers and the California Teachers Association), and others.

Whereas the major opponents leaned Democrat, one might think that Republican officeholders would have offered at least some support to Unz, but that rarely happened. Throughout Unz's campaigns, waged in four states over a period of nearly seven years, only a handful of independent-minded Republicans and even fewer Democrats spoke up in favor of his initiatives. Both parties tiptoed around his measures, probably because they assumed that Latinos opposed them, as they had California propositions 187 and 209.

Like many Democrats against Unz's California initiative, state assembly majority leader (and future mayor of Los Angeles) Antonio Villaraigoza tried to link Unz's initiative to the other two propositions: "I think the Unz initiative is the third installment in the Republican trilogy of polarizing initiatives. We will fight it." [12]

Throughout the campaign, Unz responded to attacks on himself and his initiative quickly and sharply. When an Orange County school board member accused Unz of anti–Latino racism, he noted that he had been one of the most vehement critics of Prop 187 and was a featured speaker at the huge seventy-thousand-person anti–187 rally in downtown Los Angeles, while "too many Republicans and Democrats were supporting Prop 187, or at least refusing to oppose it." [13] When questioned about his political motives, he shot back, "Some issues are liberal versus conservative. This is sanity versus insanity!" [14]

California Spanish-language radio stations, book companies, and education consultants joined together in an attempt to defeat Unz's initiative. In addition, teachers worked hard to protect the several hundred dollars per student in bilingual education that the California schools were receiving, as well as bonuses for teaching bilingual education that ranged from $3,000 to $5,000.

THE POLLS

To the surprise of people on both sides of the issue, the assumption that Latinos would oppose Unz's initiative proved wrong. In June 1997 the *Los Angeles Times* reported the results of a poll it had recently conducted showing that 83 percent of Orange County Latinos favored English-language classes for all children when starting school, while only 17 percent supported the native language instruction methods of bilingual education. Non-Latinos favored English-language instruction by 90 percent. [15]

Six months later, in early December 1997, the results of a statewide field poll of registered California voters showed less support for the Unz initiative than the earlier *Los Angeles Times* poll had, but still indicated a likely win. The respondents to the poll were read a summary of the initiative. When asked about requiring English to become the language of instruction in public school, Latinos approved by 66 percent, African Americans by 71 percent, people of Asian descent and other backgrounds by 55 percent, Democrats by 62 percent, Republicans by 76 percent, and people with other political affiliations by 71 percent. [16]

The poll respondents did have problems with some of the initiative's details. Fifty-five percent preferred that school districts, not the state, make decisions regarding the instruction of LEP students. Twenty-five percent thought that one year to learn English was sufficient, but nearly equal numbers thought it should take two or three years. [17]

When asked about the poll, a consultant hired by the California Teachers Association (CTA) and the California Association of School Administrators stated, "We're making progress." She went on to explain that many voters did not know about and would likely disapprove of the provision that teachers and administrators could be held liable for not following the particulars of the initiative. [18]

On his website, Unz explained that the numbers in the field poll were somewhat down because, unlike the *Los Angeles Times* poll, this poll included the information that the initiative would require $50 million to be spent per year for ten years to fund adult English literacy programs. He elaborated that the poll had failed to mention that on balance the initiative would save large amounts of money each year. [19]

PICKING UP STEAM

On Tuesday, December 23, 1997, Unz and his supporters received word that the initiative had officially qualified for the June ballot. More than a month earlier, they had filed petitions in excess of 700,000 signatures, of which 510,796 had been deemed valid, a number that exceeded the requirement of 433,269 signatures. In celebration of this, on January 1, 1998, Unz posted "A New Year's Resolution for California," of which the following is an excerpt:

> After years of divisive initiatives, we now have an opportunity to reunify our fractured society around "English for the Children." Reduced to a single sentence, our initiative would simply ensure that all the little immigrant children in California are sent to school and taught English so that they can become successful members of American society—which should be the most uncontroversial proposal imaginable. [20]

One week later, on January 8, 1998, State Assemblyman Mike Honda put forth Assembly Constitutional Amendment 28, a measure aimed at derailing the initiative, which was now officially called Proposition 227. It stated, "No school board should be forced by a state bureaucracy to implement an untested, unproven, arbitrarily created teaching methodology."[21] For this proposal to get on the ballot, Honda needed a two-thirds majority in both the state assembly and the state senate by January 22. The bill stalled and then died in the Assembly Education Committee.

Throughout the next few months, the polls predicted that Prop 227 would succeed easily at the polls on June 2. In reaction to this, the State Board of Education canceled bilingual education regulations and provided new guidelines that would allow school districts to design their own programs for their minority-language students.

On April 20, 1998, the state assembly passed a compromise bill, Senate Bill 6, that would create a law based on the board's new guidelines. A version of that bill had already passed the state senate nearly a year earlier but then had stalled in the assembly. According to one policy analyst, "This bill would give the voters a choice between local discretion and centralized reform."[22] Even if the bill had become law, a majority of school boards would have continued with bilingual education because of state and federal funding incentives.

Unz's former foe, Governor Pete Wilson—now a supporter of Prop 227—vetoed the bill on May 18, 1998. The governor made a statement to the state senate:

> Bilingual education in California has been a serious failure. It has done a serious disservice by keeping limited English proficient students dependent on their primary language for far too long. By denying them early fluency in

English, bilingual programs have seriously short-changed these children educationally.

Despite its purported deference to local decision making and its stated intention to create greater flexibility for implementing school districts, SB 6 in fact fails to provide much hope of improvement.[23]

BROAD MEDIA COVERAGE

Prop 227 received widespread national media attention via articles and interviews in the *Economist*, the *New York Times*, the *Chicago Tribune*, the *Washington Post*, the *Christian Science Monitor*, *Education Week*, the *Nation*, *Chicago La Raza*, *Asian Week*, *Reason* magazine, National Public Radio, and all of the California newspapers. Generally, the accounts were critical of bilingual education while at the same time leery that Prop 227 would go too far.

The *Wall Street Journal* quoted Latinos in favor of the initiative, then explained that it was not clear whether ending bilingual education would help or hurt the children. In the same article, Professor Catherine Snow of the Harvard College of Education was quoted as disapproving of the initiative. She predicted the students "will end up with poorer literacy skills and more disaffected from society than they are now."[24]

Calling Prop 227 the "Son of 187," William Wong, columnist for the *San Francisco Examiner*, said that bilingual education did not need "an assault weapon approach." He was critical that the English immersion classes would hold back students from receiving instruction in core subjects and that Prop 227 did not address children over ten years old who still needed language support.[25]

In general, the media criticized Prop 227 for designating a time limit to learn English "not normally intended to exceed one year," requiring $5 million per year spent on adult English instruction, specifying that parents could bring lawsuits against school board members and other elected officials for intentionally not following the law, creating a one-size-fits-all program for all schools, and allowing children to fall behind in content-area subjects because they would no longer be allowed instruction in their native language.

Occasionally a media outlet told about a successful bilingual education program. For the most part, however, the news stories concerned children who had been segregated for several years and not taught enough English to ever become competitive with their English-speaking peers. On the other hand, education experts warned frequently that without bilingual education, English learners would lose enthusiasm, not want to attend school, and fall even more behind academically.

THE LAST LAP OF THE CAMPAIGN

The political atmosphere around Prop 227 became especially heated in the last couple months of the campaign. There were protests, criticisms from President Bill Clinton, disparaging remarks from the US Secretary of Education, and last minute donations of huge sums of money to both sides.

On April 22, 1998, about two thousand students from high schools in the Bay Area left their classrooms in the morning to protest the provisions of propositions 187, 209, and 227. The members of Voices of Struggle had organized the teenagers to take a stand against racial intolerance. Fortunately, the students were well behaved, with the exception of single incidents of fruit throwing and rock tossing.[26]

At a public forum held at the University of California, Irvine, on April 26, 1998, a fourteen-member panel from the *Harvard Educational Review* discussed Prop 227. They all agreed that LEP students would suffer should the initiative pass. José Moreno, a member of the Harvard board, stated that it would be a setback for California children because it offered "a singular model to a diverse population."[27]

On April 29, 1998, Unz squared off with Holli Thier, chief spokesperson in opposition to the measure, before a crowd of 250 people at a televised public forum in Contra Costa. Unz talked about the failings of the present bilingual education system and Thier called his plan "an educational straitjacket" that would take away decision making from the local schools. Fifteen minutes into the forum, about fifteen young people stood up and refused to sit down. Security guards had to escort them out of the room. Unz noted that such hostility toward him was usual at such events.[28]

Clinton criticized Prop 227 at a Democratic fund-raiser on May 1, 1998, stating that Prop 227 set "rigid and unrealistic deadlines." He said that the measure would "consign countless children of immigrants to a lifetime of 'intellectual purgatory.'"[29] A few days earlier, US Secretary of Education Richard Riley had called it "a disaster," "counterproductive," and "just plain wrong."[30]

On May 20, 1998, Los Angeles mayor Richard Riordan, a Republican, contributed $250,000 of his own money to put an ad on Spanish-language television in favor of Prop 227; it would run three hundred times leading up to Election Day. He had already gained support from Latinos by donating to education programs, many of them beneficial to Latinos, over a span of several years.[31]

In late May 1998 billionaire A. Jerrold Perenchio, chairman and chief executive of Univision Communications Incorporated, the largest Spanish-language television network in the nation, contributed $650,000 to the CTA to help the organization defeat the initiative. Altogether, the CTA was able to buy $2.7 million in television time statewide, with the latest ad featuring the four major candidates for governor as opposing Prop 227.[32] At the same time, Perenchio was running anti–Proposition 227 editorials on his Spanish-language stations four times daily, without representation from the other side.[33]

A spokesperson for Unz explained, "Perenchio is certainly placing financial gain ahead of children's interests by attempting to ensure that Latino children do not learn English for many, many years. His large contribution makes it clear that it would be bad for his profits if children [were] to learn English."[34]

VICTORY

On June 2, 1998, California's Prop 227 won a landslide victory at the polls with 61 percent of the vote. Unz rejoiced at his press conference:

> We overcame enormous odds to win this victory. Our initiative was opposed by the President of the United States. The Chairman of the state Republican Party and the chair of the state Democratic Party opposed it. It was opposed by all four candidates for Governor, Democrat and Republican alike. It was opposed by nearly all the state's major newspapers and virtually every educational organization, large union, and establishment group. Our only strong support came from the people of California, but that was enough for victory.[35]

According to the California Fair Political Practices Commission (FPPC), Unz had raised and spent $1,250,000 for his campaign. The bulk of the campaign money was used for gathering the nearly eight hundred thousand signatures needed to qualify the initiative for the ballot.[36]

The opposition had raised and spent about $4.4 million, mostly on advertising and voter contact. Two smaller committees had raised and spent another $50,000. In addition, the free airtime for editorials protesting Prop 227 provided by Perenchio on Univision was estimated to be worth $1 to $2 million.[37]

This was the first victory of its kind in the United States. Citizen Ron Unz had successfully used the political process to almost singlehandedly eliminate a federally funded, California-mandated program that had proven detrimental to the education of children whose first language was not English. And he had only just begun!

Chapter Two

Under Attack

The Unz initiative was carefully constructed to withstand litigation. In May 1998, shortly before the passage of the California measure, President Bill Clinton's White House legal analysts concluded that the provisions of Proposition 227 would not violate any federal civil rights laws and therefore were unlikely to be struck down in court. The analysts elaborated that the intensive English immersion program of Prop 227 was fully consistent with *Lau v. Nichols*, the constitutional basis for what was considered to be bilingual education by the US Supreme Court in 1974. [1]

The ruling of the US Court of Appeals for the Ninth Circuit in *Guadalupe v. Tempe* (1978) states that bilingual education is not required under either the US Constitution or the 1964 Civil Rights Act, so providing extra English language assistance satisfies the requirement of *Lau v. Nichols*. [2] Nevertheless, foes of Prop 227 pursued costly litigation and other means to render the new law based on the Unz initiative null and void.

VALERIA G. ET AL. V. WILSON ET AL.

On June 3, 1998, one day after the California Prop 227 victory, a lawsuit in opposition to the initiative was filed in federal court in San Francisco. It claimed that Prop 227 provisions violated the Equal Educational Opportunities Act (EEOA) by imposing "an experimental instructional program" on LEP California students, without regard to their individual needs.

The plaintiffs were made up of several mostly left-leaning groups:

- Multicultural Education, Training and Advocacy (META) Inc.;
- the American Civil Liberties Union;

- Hispanic activist groups, including the Mexican American Legal Defense and Educational Fund, Parents for Unity, Mujeres Unidas y Activas, Chinese for Affirmative Action, and the California Latino Civil Rights Network;
- the Los Angeles Unified School District and the Educational Alliance for the California School Boards Association; and
- the California Rural Legal Assistance Foundation, representing students, which filed amicus briefs in support of the plaintiffs' motion for preliminary injunction, an order to prohibit the implementation of Prop 227.

The defense argued that immersion methods were not experimental in that they had been successfully implemented for many years in Canada, Europe, and Israel. Moreover, the third waiver allowed exemptions for students with special needs.

The defense was made up of two groups:

- Governor Pete Wilson, the California State Board of Education, and State Superintendent of Public Instruction Delaine Eastin; and
- Supporters of Proposition 227, including Ron Unz, Rosalie Pedalino Porter, Gloria Matta Tuchman, and Linda Chavez, president of the Center for Equal Opportunity.

On July 15, 1998, Federal District Judge Charles Legge ruled in favor of the initiative. He stated that the immersion program of Prop 227 was pedagogically sound and was what the people of California preferred, as proved by their votes. He agreed with the defendants that students with special needs were provided for through the third waiver: the child already has been placed for a period of not less than thirty days during that school year in an English language classroom and it is subsequently the informed belief of the school principal and educational staff that the child has such special physical, emotional, psychological, or educational needs that an alternate course of educational study would be better suited to the child's overall educational development. He found no legal basis for requiring bilingual education.[3]

The plaintiffs pursued two appeals over the next four years, losing both of them. On February 25, 2003, the Ninth Circuit Court denied their third and final request for yet another hearing.

CALIFORNIA TEACHERS ASSOCIATION ET AL. V. STATE BOARD OF EDUCATION

On December 4, 1998, the California Teachers Association and other professional organizations filed a petition in federal court for an injunction against the section of Prop 227 that gave parents the right to sue school officials for willfully and repeatedly refusing to implement the terms of the statute. The plaintiffs claimed that the proposition provision was vague and that it would violate the constitutional rights to free speech and due process.

On September 8, 1999, US Federal District Judge Edward Rafeedie ruled that the personal liability provision allowing parents to sue school officials for not following the provisions of the proposition was constitutional, adding that teachers were not prohibited from using "languages other than English in disciplining students, emergency training, social interactions, tutoring, parent-teacher conferences, or any of the other situations listed by the plaintiffs."[4] The plaintiffs appealed twice to the Ninth Circuit Court and lost both times.

FEDERAL COURT RULING REGARDING SAN JOSÉ SCHOOLS

On December 16, 1998, US District Judge Ronald M. Whyte gave the San José Unified School District permission to continue its bilingual education program throughout its sixteen elementary schools. Unlike the other California school districts, San José was under a federal court order that required it to desegregate its schools and offer native language instruction to Spanish-speaking students. According to San José superintendent Linda Murray, the district had worked very hard to minimize conflict with state law and the court order.[5]

According to the agreement made with the court, the parents and not the school administration would decide whether an LEP student was to be placed in a bilingual program. The parents would have to visit the school, attend information meetings, and sign waivers annually. However, the students would not be required to spend their first thirty days in an English immersion program, a requirement of Prop 227.[6]

As noted by Mike Hersher, general counsel for the California Department of Education, and reiterated by Ron Unz, this ruling would not affect the other districts because other districts were not under the court order. Unz added, "[Judge Whyte] made the decision based on the assumption that the program was working well, and it's not."[7]

MCLAUGHLIN V. CALIFORNIA STATE BOARD OF EDUCATION

Several San Francisco–area school districts wanted to obtain waivers that would allow them exemption from the waiver provisions of Prop 227. In this challenge, justices of the California Court of Appeal, First Appellate District, in San Francisco decided on September 27, 1999, that only parents could request waivers.

On February 25, 2000, California Attorney General Bill Lockyer added his own ruling to the appellate court decision: "A school district may not deny a parental request for an individual waiver from the statutory mandate that all students be instructed in English on the sole ground that the district has no alternative program."[8] Bilingual education advocate and author James Crawford agreed with the attorney general's decision: "The parents' right to choose bilingual education, even after Proposition 227, was reaffirmed."[9]

COMPLAINT FROM THE CALIFORNIA DEPARTMENT OF EDUCATION

Oceanside Unified School District superintendent Ken Noonan, one of the original founders of the California Association for Bilingual Education, had opposed Prop 227 but had nevertheless implemented the provisions of the initiative to the nth degree. After two years of immersion instruction, the mean percentile test scores of his district's immigrant children soared. Noonan noticed other positive changes, such as ELLs mixing more frequently than before with their English-only peers on the playground.[10] As a result, he became a staunch supporter of immersion education.

Because of Oceanside's rising test scores, the district had become the focus of national media coverage in the *New York Times*, the *Washington Post*, *USA Today*, the *Wall Street Journal*, *Newsweek*, and national television networks. The district was described as the one that had most thoroughly implemented Prop 227 (see chap. 3, pp. 34–36).

Nevertheless, in October 2000, Oceanside Unified School District came under fire from the California Department of Education and the federal Office for Civil Rights (OCR). The district was forced to defend itself against a claim that the district was restricting LEP children from access to alternative programs such as bilingual education. This was in response to a complaint filed in July 1999 by META and California Rural Legal Assistance on behalf of the United Coalition for the Education of Our Children, a group of parents seeking continued Spanish-language instruction for their children.

Unz lambasted the Department of Education for its action:

> California Superintendent Delaine Eastin and all of the pro-bilingual fanatics in her Department of Education were fervent opponents of Proposition 227, and the people of California crushed them at the polls in 1998. Now they are claiming black is white and they want to punish Oceanside Superintendent Ken Noonan for obeying the law and doubling his students' test scores as a result.
>
> Perhaps if Noonan had managed to triple his test scores, they would have tried to arrest him. Punishing a California district for its academic success shows everyone in America why our state's scores dropped to dead last in the

country during the 1980s. This is the craziest thing since Stalinist Russia arrested its peasant farmers if they worked too hard. [11]

Noonan said that the report had omitted the improved performance of his LEP students: "If you read the report it sounds like our students are in a deep dark hole." [12] He appealed the report and eventually was able to work out a solution with the state and the OCR.

Admired by his colleagues for his accomplishments and willingness to find solutions, Noonan was named Superintendent of the Year by the California Association of Latino Superintendents in 2002.

POLITICAL ACTION AT THE BILINGUAL EDUCATION CONFERENCE

Governor Gray Davis had nominated former principal Nancy Ichinaga to the California Board of Education in 2000. On February 7, 2001, the California State Senate Rules Committee was scheduled to decide whether to recommend her appointment for a full vote in the senate.

No one expected there to be a problem with Ichinaga's confirmation. Her policies had brought about impressive academic achievement at Bennett-Kew Elementary School in Inglewood, California, an elementary school attended predominantly by at-risk, poverty-stricken children. The home language of approximately 50 percent of the students was Spanish.

By implementing a systematic phonics-based reading program and eliminating bilingual education—both practices considered illegal in California at the time—Ichinaga had fully transformed this poor-performing low-income school into one of the highest performers in all of Los Angeles County. Nevertheless, due to the school's noncompliance with state law that required bilingual education for limited English proficient (LEP) children, the school had almost lost its federal Title I funding designated for these children's instruction. As the school's test scores soared and its Hispanic students became proficient in English, Ichinaga received a waiver from the California Department of Education, which she referred to as an "achievement based excuse." [13]

At the January 2001 California Association for Bilingual Education Annual Conference in Los Angeles, the nearly twenty thousand participants were encouraged to oppose Ichinaga's appointment. Each attendee was provided with a magenta-colored flyer that contained the urgent message in bold, black letters: "Action Alert: Stop Ichinaga's Appointment to the State Board of Education!" Ichinaga was then described as an opponent of bilingual education and supporter of Prop 227. No mention was made of her accomplishments at Bennett-Kew Elementary School.

The flyer listed the telephone numbers, e-mails, and addresses of the members of the State Senate Rules Committee who would vote on Ichinaga's appointment. The attendees were directed to go to a specific area of the conference hall where computers were available for them to contact the specified state senators.

The resulting barrage of letters and phone calls to the state senators stalled the vote for one week. Meanwhile, newspaper reporters throughout California learned what had happened and informed the public about the CABE conference attendees' campaign to undermine Ichinaga's appointment. An overwhelming response in favor of Ichinaga resulted.

On February 22, 2001, following approval from the State Senate Rules Committee, the full California State Senate confirmed Nancy Ichinaga's appointment to the California Board of Education by a unanimous vote of 29 to 0.

THE CALIFORNIA BOARD OF EDUCATION'S ATTEMPT TO UNDO PROP 227

A year later, on February 7, 2002, the California Board of Education proposed regulations that had the potential to dismantle Prop 227. One regulation eliminated the requirement that all "English language learners (ELLs)"—the newly accepted term for LEP students—under ten years old spend the first thirty days of every school year in an English-language program before being allowed to qualify for a waiver to go into bilingual programs. Another regulation gave teachers the right to apply for and be granted waivers so they could assign the students to bilingual education classes as they saw fit. In response to outrage from the media and the public, the board eliminated its last imposed regulation on April 25, 2002.

ASSEMBLY BILL 2711

In the meantime, Assemblyman Mark Wyland introduced Assembly Bill 2711, which disallowed anyone from overtly recruiting parents to request waivers and mandated a written description of a legitimate educational reason for granting a waiver. The bill also required the State Department of Education to monitor and enforce the language in the proposition that required ELLs to learn English by being in English-speaking classrooms.

On April 24, 2002, Assembly Bill 2711 was heard in the Assembly Committee on Education with testimonies from Unz and Noonan. However, according to a report by Noonan and Wyland that ran in the *San Diego Union-Tribune*, "Succumbing to pressure from the bilingual and teachers' union lobbies, the committee's Democratic majority voted to kill the bill."[14]

PROGRAMS IGNORE THE PROVISIONS OF PROP 227

Bilingual education advocates claimed that Prop 227 took away the rights of the parents. However, there was no evidence that parents of ELLs had ever been given much choice regarding the education of their children, according to Boston University professor Christine H. Rossell, who had analyzed data collected from her visits to more than three hundred classrooms between 1986 and 2001.

In her article "The Near End of Bilingual Education," Rossell concluded that California teachers had remained the "primary decision makers" as to whether or not a child was put into bilingual education. She likened the situation to medical care: "Teachers, like doctors, create supply by the criteria they use to define a child as needing treatment and they create demand by telling the patient what treatment he or she needs."

Rossell elaborated further that in every California school she visited in the spring of 1999, teachers admitted that they had "worked very hard" to get parents to sign waivers. The teachers had held meetings and called parents "to persuade them that their child would be better off in the bilingual-education program."[15]

Rossell's research showed that the California State Board of Education had allowed school districts to follow guidelines that contradicted the provisions of Prop 227:

- What was described in the initiative as a "sheltered English immersion classroom" had become redefined. [*Note: Sheltered English immersion* is the broader term for *structured English immersion.*] The school districts considered such classrooms to be not only ones in which English learners were taught in English at a pace they could understand, but also "mainstream classrooms with English as a Second Language (ESL) pullout instruction and self-contained classrooms of English Learners receiving up to 30 percent of their instruction in Spanish."
- Teachers had been permitted to recruit children for bilingual classrooms, although the proposition clearly stated that parents were supposed to initiate this process.
- Parents had been allowed to mail in requests for waivers instead of visiting the schools, as the measure required.
- The Prop 227 requirement that English learners spend a year in a sheltered immersion classroom (SEI) was unilaterally changed by the State Board of Education from a maximum (the initiative stated, "not normally intended to exceed one year")[16] to a minimum time period. Consequently, a student could be allowed to stay in a sheltered program for years, even if the child was no longer benefiting from it.

- Documentation of the need for bilingual education was required in the initiative, but this requirement was ignored by many school districts.
- According to many supporters of the measure—including Christine Rossell, Rosalie Pedalino Porter, and Ron Unz—the State Board of Education's interpretation of vague parts of the legislation subverted the intent of Prop 227. Whereas the legislation required LEP children to spend thirty days in an English-language classroom, the Board of Education decided that this would occur only at the time of the child's first enrollment as an LEP student in a California school. The Prop 227 authors had intended the thirty-day time period to transpire every year for students still in bilingual education.[17]

SHELTERED ENGLISH IMMERSION MOSTLY REPLACES BILINGUAL EDUCATION

Immediately after the passage of Prop 227, some California school districts chose to either change or ignore the provisions of the new law. At the same time, starting in 1998 a growing majority of districts adopted SEI programs. This led to a steady decline in bilingual education programs throughout the state. Whereas 29 percent of all LEP students were enrolled in bilingual education during the 1997–1998 school year, fewer than 10 percent were enrolled during the 2001–2002 school year. The trend was clearly moving away from native language instruction.[18]

After 1998, 35 percent of the California ELLs learned in an SEI setting in the 2000–2001 school year, 50 percent in 2004–2005, and 55 percent, in 2008–2009. Figures from the California English Learner Services Report indicate that only approximately 7 percent of ELLs were receiving bilingual instruction in the 2004–2005 school year, and by 2008–2009 that number had fallen to 5 percent.[19]

The decline of bilingual education continued every year thereafter as it was replaced by various forms of SEI. This change in approach achieved the stated goal of Prop 227: Students gained English language skills rapidly and effectively to the extent that they were able to be moved into mainstream classrooms and participate in equal educational opportunity.

According to the National Center for Education Statistics, in spite of an overall increase in the number of immigrant children in California schools during that same period, the total number of ELLs dropped from 1.416 million in 2011–2012[20] to 1.332 million in 2015–2016.[21] The Spanish speakers made up the largest group, at 83 percent; speakers of Vietnamese comprised the second largest language group, at 2.14 percent.[22]

Whereas California had been responsible for educating as many as 50 percent of the entire ELL population in the United States for several years, that figure had dropped to 24.5 percent by 2013, according to the Migration Policy Institute.[23] Large numbers of California schoolchildren had become "reclassified fluent English proficient" students and were no longer in need of special English language services.

In fact, a whopping 33 percent of ELLs in California achieved English language proficiency every year, on average, from school years 2007–2008 to 2014–2015, an impressive improvement over the 5 percent who had achieved proficiency in 1995.[24] Between the school years 2007–2008 to 2012–2013, California's monitored former limited English proficient (MFLEP) students who had been reclassified and mainstreamed for one to two years scored proficient in reading every year at an average rate of 62.1 percent, while 59.2 percent was the average rate over the same period for *all students* in California. The same MFLEP students outscored all students in reaching math proficiency during that time on average by nearly 6 percentage points (61 percent, compared to 55.1 percent). [*Note:* It was not possible to compute state test score comparisons after 2013 because of missing data for MFLEP students.][25]

Sixty-nine percent of the ELLs graduated from high school in 2015, nearly 4 percentage points above the national average for ELLs.[26] [*Note:* Undoubtedly, the rate would be considerably higher had the former ELLs been included.]

PROPOSITION 58

With these reported achievements of ELLs throughout California since the passage of Prop 227 in 1998, it defies reason that Californians would vote to revert to the failed bilingual education policies of the last century. Unfortunately, that happened at the ballot box on November 8, 2016, when California voters approved Prop 58 with a 73.5 percent majority vote. This ballot measure rescinds Prop 227, authorizing schools to implement bilingual education, specifically dual-language programs. Consequently, ELLs at any public school may end up spending 50 to 80 percent of their school time being taught their major school subjects in their native language, rather than in English, in accordance with a grossly damaging educational approach that was a documented failure in California for two decades.

Prop 58 was promoted as a means to provide children the opportunity to graduate from high school with proficiency in two languages—a fraudulent, illogical claim that was unquestioningly accepted by well-intentioned voters. This new law, if funded and aggressively implemented, will weaken the education of immigrant children, who have been making great strides in mastering English and becoming successful in mainstream classes. Moreover, it will not live up to its romantic ideal that a substantial number of students will become functionally fluent and literate in two languages by the time they graduate from California high schools.

Unfortunately, the average voter is not aware of the issues involved with educating children who do not know the common language of the school and the community. As the state with the highest number of ELLs, California will be putting at risk a large proportion of the entire ELL population in the United States.

Chapter Three

Latinos vs. Latinos

The Arizona Language War

Maria Mendoza had followed California's English for the Children campaign for several months, and she was jubilant when her sister called her early in the morning of June 3, 1998, to inform her that Proposition 227 had passed by a landslide. In Mendoza's opinion, bilingual education was the single most negative factor in the education of Hispanic students.[1] She hoped something could be done about it in Arizona, where she had lived for forty-one years.

In the 1960s Mendoza singlehandedly disputed the bilingual education policies of the Tucson Unified School District (TUSD), eventually suing the school district based on her strong objections to what she had witnessed in the classroom and had heard from parents.

As a bilingual instructional aide at a TUSD school, she was required to translate lessons into Spanish for children who did not understand English. As a result, the children did not pay attention to the English, because they knew Mendoza would explain everything in Spanish. Having learned English herself as a small child in a school in New Mexico, she knew this was not a good way to teach English to Hispanic children.[2]

In 1965 Mendoza went before the TUSD Governing Board, representing Spanish-speaking parents who wanted their children removed from bilingual education classes because they were not learning to speak and read English. When nothing came of her efforts, she took her case before the Arizona State Board of Education. That action proved futile as well.

Finally, in 1974, Mendoza initiated the lawsuit *Mendoza v. Tucson Unified School District #1.* When she won the judgment in 1978, school officials were no longer allowed to put children into bilingual education classes without their parents' knowledge and consent.

However, according to Mendoza, the stipulation was not being honored: TUSD school officials were not notifying the parents. When parents requested that their children be taken out of the bilingual classes, school authorities tried to change the parents' minds with the threat that the school would not be held responsible for ensuring their children learned to read and write English if they were removed from those classes.[3]

It did not take much thought for Mendoza to decide to start a movement similar to the one that had just succeeded in California. However, she realized she could not do it alone.

FINDING AND ORGANIZING SUPPORTERS

Mendoza telephoned high school teacher Hector Ayala, whom she had recently talked to concerning a commentary he had written for the *Tucson Citizen*. He had taken to task a TUSD official for blaming the low achievement of Hispanic students on the lack of a Mexican-American studies program. Ayala instead believed bilingual education was responsible.

Ayala had learned English in school after his family had moved from Mexico to Nogales, Arizona, when he was nine years old. He recalled how he and several of his classmates from Mexico had picked up English at a good pace by being immersed in the language. He believed there was no excuse for so many children to not learn English.

Ayala agreed to help Mendoza dismantle bilingual education in Arizona. He talked some friends into helping him create flyers that publicized the movement and a future meeting. He posted them on telephone poles and car windshields, in shopping malls, and in other highly visible places in Tucson's predominantly Hispanic neighborhoods. Hundreds of people, many of them parents, expressed their support for the anti–bilingual education cause. Their enthusiasm convinced him that Mendoza and he were on the right track.[4]

Mendoza and Ayala held meetings in churches and homes to inform the public about the purpose of their cause. Turnout was meager at first: only six or seven people. But soon that number increased to ten, then twelve, and ultimately fifty. It was not until their fifth or sixth meeting that opponents began to appear. Education professors and VIPs such as Ken and Ute Goodman, originators of the controversial Whole Language reading program, came to oppose their efforts. The gatherings soon morphed into shouting matches—and even worse.

Once, after Ayala stepped into his car to leave one of the meetings, a man pounded on his window and shouted, "I know where you live now, mother f——!" After another meeting, he discovered that his car had been sandpapered. People shouted and carried signs with the words *vendido* (sellout), *coconut, racist*, and other insults directed at him.[5] Such harassment continued throughout the campaign. Mendoza and Ayala had to become discreet about when and where they held their meetings, as well as whom they invited.

By July 1998 a small circle of enthusiastic, committed supporters had evolved. Mendoza decided to take the next step and connect with Ron Unz, whom she reached, after many tries, by telephone. When she explained that she wanted to create an Arizona initiative similar to Proposition 227, he agreed to contribute both financial and legal assistance.[6]

Unz traveled to Tucson that July and met with seven core members of the movement. He explained that they could run a low-cost campaign by handing out flyers, writing letters to newspapers, doing interviews, and speaking to forums across the state. Mendoza and Ayala expressed their concern that meetings were drawing people from organizations advocating immigration reform and English-only laws. After some discussion, the group decided to exclude those with motives other than dismantling bilingual education, refusing to accept their donations.[7]

THE MOVEMENT SPREADS TO THE PHOENIX AREA

In early August, Margaret Garcia Dugan and Norma Alvarez attended one of Mendoza and Ayala's Tucson meetings. The women worked in Glendale, a town with a large Hispanic community that borders northwest Phoenix; both had grown up in Spanish-speaking families.

As principal of Glendale High School for eight years, Dugan had been recognized nationally for her leadership skills and successful program for limited English proficient students. Dugan had found that the Hispanic students who had learned English through immersion methods in elementary school were considerably better prepared for high school than those who had been enrolled in bilingual programs. She wanted to do something about this discrepancy.[8]

Dugan's friend Norma Alvarez, a social worker for the city of Glendale, had been a supporter of bilingual education until the early 1980s, when she was stunned to discover that her own son Jeff, a third grader who spoke only English, had been put in a bilingual program. Her determination to pull her son out of the program angered the school officials, who insisted the boy would fail miserably without it.

With the help of Rosie Lopez, the wife of state senator Joe Eddie Lopez who later became an advocate for bilingual education, Alvarez was able to have her son transferred into a mainstream class. After that, Alvarez helped other parents have their children removed from bilingual classes.

Years later, Jeff Alvarez, now a medical doctor, recalled that most of his classmates in elementary school had been from Spanish-speaking homes and were enrolled in bilingual education. He had progressed because he was fluent in English at the time he entered school. Often he acted as a tutor to those students who were struggling with English.

According to Dr. Alvarez, "The students in bilingual education could not speak English any better at the end of eighth grade than they could in the early grades." He believed strongly that if those students had been immersed in English in the early grades, their academic achievement would have been much greater.[9]

After attending Mendoza and Ayala's Tucson meeting, Dugan and Norma Alvarez arranged their own invitation-only gatherings for people in the Phoenix-Glendale area, usually held in the refurbished garage at Alvarez's home. The twenty to thirty participants who attended regularly were mostly Latino parents. The women kept in contact with Mendoza and Ayala, talking to one or the other on the telephone every other night throughout the campaign.

During his second trip to Arizona in mid-August 1998, Ron Unz helped Ayala and Mendoza turn their Tucson homes into offices for the movement, complete with fax and copy machines as well as additional phone lines, which rang constantly as the campaign intensified. Unz met with Dugan and a lawyer in Phoenix who could give advice on how to word their initiative in accordance with Arizona law. Together, Dugan and Unz figured out the particulars, which Unz later discussed and finalized with the lawyer.[10]

Mendoza became the official statewide chairperson. Ayala, Dugan, and Norma Alvarez acted as cochairs of their new organization: English for the Children—Arizona.

THE ARIZONA INITIATIVE

Like California Proposition 227, the Arizona initiative stated that all children in each of the state's public schools "shall be taught English by being taught in English and all children shall be placed in English language classrooms." It allowed for the same three waivers and mandated sheltered English immersion for a time period "not normally intended to exceed one year."

However, the Arizona initiative broadened the definition of a child who already knows English as one "who already possesses good English language skills, as measured by *oral evaluation or* standardized tests of English vocabulary comprehension, reading, and writing, in which the child scores at or above the state average for his or her grade level or at or above the 5th grade average, whichever is lower."[11] After the initiative became law, the three-word addition "oral evaluation or" to the original California measure gave the bilingual education advocates in Arizona an excuse for circumventing the measure (see chap. 4, p. 41).

Unlike Prop 227, the Arizona initiative did not fund adult English language instruction. Moreover, it demanded more punitive action than Prop 227 against those who were guilty of "willfully and repeatedly" not implementing the law: "Any individual found so liable shall be immediately removed from office, and shall be barred from holding any position of authority anywhere within the Arizona public school system for an additional period of five years."[12]

In addition, unlike Prop 227, the Arizona measure stated that "teachers and local school districts may reject waiver requests without explanation or legal consequences."[13] This prerogative imposed "virtually air-tight restrictions on the use of native-language instruction in public schools,"[14] according to bilingual education advocate and author James Crawford.

When Unz was interviewed on KVOA in Tucson on August 14, he explained, "If something hasn't worked after twenty to thirty years, it is time to try something different." He added that according to statistics, very few bilingual education students were being mainstreamed each year and that children in other language groups who were not in bilingual classes had made much better progress in learning English.[15]

On the same telecast, bilingual education advocates explained that bilingual education works when done right, but that some programs needed to be improved. They said that it would be a mistake to get rid of all programs, because without them, many students would be lost in class and not progress as they should.[16]

REGISTERING THE INITIATIVE

On January 6, 1999, Maria Mendoza, Hector Ayala, Ron Unz, about ten supporters, and a few children appeared at the El Rio Neighborhood Center in Tucson. Their purpose was to announce their intent to register the initiative at the secretary of state's office in Phoenix later that day.

A crowd of about one hundred irate demonstrators had gathered at the center. Many held signs high that read "Unz go home" while shouting those words repeatedly in unison. Some sign-waving bilingual education backers called the proposition's proponents Ku Klux Klan members and child abusers. The proponents of the measure were forced against a wall, and a few of the accompanying children who were wearing English for the Children T-shirts sobbed while their parents and grandparents hugged them. The children were finally led away from the ruckus.[17]

After the crowd had settled down, Ayala read from his prepared text: "Hispanic students have been relegated to lowly positions in our society because of bilingual education's gross inability to educate them adequately."[18] He elaborated that his group felt encouraged that their initiative would succeed.

Later that afternoon, the English for the Children officers drove 125 miles to Phoenix and filed their paperwork at the Arizona State Capitol without incident.

POOR ACHIEVEMENT

On February 1, 1999, Arizona superintendent of public instruction Lisa Graham Keegan presented her report to the state legislature regarding the bilingual and English as a second language programs for school year 1997–1998. LEP children comprised about 15 percent of the entire school population, and only about 4 percent of the 112,522 LEP population had learned enough English to be reclassified as fluent English proficient (FEP), according to the results of the English proficiency tests. The school districts, the state, and the federal government had invested more than $361 million, beyond the usual school funding, into the education of these children.

State Senator Joe Eddie Lopez blamed the low results on the state education officials who he said had failed to monitor the programs. He went on to state, "These programs do work, and they [the officials] are mandated to make them work and try to correct failures, and they have not."[19]

INCONCLUSIVE DATA

The schools in Arizona, unlike the ones in California, were not required by law to implement bilingual education approaches for instructing LEP students. Many schools chose programs that consisted of variations or combinations of bilingual education and/or ESL.

The Arizona Department of Education (ADE) could not analyze whether bilingual education worked better or worse than ESL. According to Keegan's cover letter in her report to the legislature, schools and districts were submitting "conflicting information, causing confusion and making analysis difficult."[20] Moreover, in spite of three deadline extensions, 40 percent of the schools had sent their data in too late to be analyzed for the report.[21]

Although it was questionable, the data gave the achievement edge to bilingual education. The students identified by the schools to be learning through bilingual techniques had scored higher than those in ESL programs on the standardized, nationally norm-referenced Stanford 9 Achievement Test (SAT-9) in which the 50th percentile was the national norm. The bilingual education students scored at the 23rd to 25th percentiles on the reading portion and at the 20th to 23rd percentiles on the language segment. The scores for ESL students were at the 18th percentile on both sections.[22]

These figures lacked reliability, however. The data listed the very large Phoenix Union High School District as ESL although most of its schools offered LEP students content-area classes in Spanish. In addition, the teachers were not restricted in any way from using Spanish while teaching ESL. Only in a few districts were the LEP students taught predominantly in English.

Moreover, many bilingual education students took advantage of the three-year exemption from the SAT-9 and instead took the Aprenda, the Spanish version of the test. The result was that a small, elite percentage of bilingual education students were compared on the SAT-9 to a majority of the ESL population.

INITIATIVE TO REMEDY PROBLEMS

Joe Eddie Lopez often complained that training for the teachers of LEP students was inadequate and should be addressed. He stated that about three thousand (later reported to be fewer than twenty-five hundred[23]) teachers of bilingual education did not have the proper training and credentials.[24]

There were several other reasons for the LEP students' low achievement:

- Perverse monetary incentive. Districts would lose federal and state funds once the children were reclassified as FEP, a requirement for mainstreaming.
- Proficiency tests were often unreasonably difficult. Only 47 percent of English-only students were likely to score "English proficient" on the reading portion of the Language Assessment Scales (LAS),[25] one of the most reputable and popular English proficiency tests at the time. Other tests demanded even higher standards for exit out of an English language acquisition program.
- Segregation. LEP students were frequently taught in a setting separate from their English-dominant peers for most of the day. As a result, they spoke their native language often to each other—and, when speaking English, reinforced among themselves English language errors common to their language group.
- High mobility rate. The families of LEP students tended to move frequently. As a result, students could end up in classes that were too difficult for them or be required to repeat what they had already learned. No attempt had been made to standardize their instruction.

- Literacy problems. English-fluent LEP students were taught lessons meant for children learning English, when in actuality they needed intense remediation in reading.
- Inadequate teacher training. Prospective teachers learned mostly simplistic, "natural" approaches. Colleges of education offered little or no guidance on how to teach important elements of English grammar and vocabulary sequentially.
- Excessive use of Spanish. To various degrees, LEP students—whether formally in bilingual education or not—received a great deal of their instruction in Spanish.

The passage of the anti–bilingual education initiative would guarantee not only that the LEP students—specifically those under the age of ten—would be immersed in English, but also that they would learn through SEI, a systematic method that would bring rigor and continuity to their instruction. Because their time in the program would be limited to a period "normally not to exceed a year," LEP students would no longer languish in remedial programs year after year.

CONFLICTS IN THE LEGISLATURE

In the early months of 1998, when California Prop 227 was gaining momentum, Arizona State Representative Laura Knaperek introduced House Bill 2532, which limited funding for Arizona bilingual and ESL programs to a total of four years per individual student.

Leonardo Basurto, TUSD bilingual education director, said that Knaperek's bill would cause TUSD to lose as much as $750,000 in funding every year. He explained that approximately seventy-five hundred of his district's LEP students, out of approximately ten thousand total, had been in bilingual and ESL programs for more than four years. He stated that it took four to seven years to master a language, according to some research.[26]

HB 2532 passed in the state house, but did not come to a vote in the senate, due mostly to the efforts of Joe Eddie Lopez, who planned to sponsor his own bill in early 1999, which he said would be endorsed "by most of the education establishment."[27]

Lopez's bill would have required schools to pay certified bilingual education teachers $2,000 per year above their regular salaries and to reimburse them for the cost of acquiring their bilingual education or ESL certificates. LEP students would be excused from having to pass the Arizona Instrument to Measure Standards (AIMS), which was a requirement for graduation from high school.

In April 1999, in response to Arizona's English for the Children movement and Lopez's proposed bill, Knaperek introduced House Bill 2387, which restricted the funding to three years rather than four. Like Lopez's bill, it provided a system for evaluating programs and allowed parents the opportunity to choose the appropriate program for their children.

Lopez would not agree to the three-year limit and dismissed the concerns of other legislators that the anti–bilingual education initiative would be successful: "Of course I do not believe they [voters] will pass the initiative. Passing the bill has nothing to do with the initiative."[28] Lopez succeeded in killing Knaperek's bill.[29]

Knaperek had no choice but to revise HB 2387 so that it did not limit bilingual education or ESL in any way. The new bill required schools to notify parents of their children's placement in the programs, allowed the parents to opt out of them, and created a legislative committee to study the issue. The bill passed in that form and Governor Jane Hull signed it.

Arizona Republic columnist Ruben Navarrette Jr. described what had occurred: "By letting pettiness, personal ambition and political opportunism get in the way of mending a flawed program, the Legislature has all but ensured the success of a proposed ballot initiative that would end it altogether."[30]

According to Navarrette, if Knaperek's original HB 2387 had passed, it might have stopped the momentum of the anti–bilingual education initiative, which would have been a good thing in the eyes of the Republicans. Because it had not passed, the Democrats now hoped that they could scare the Hispanic voters into showing up and rejecting the initiative at the ballot box.

Mendoza, chair of the Arizona anti–bilingual education movement, called the bill a "'worthless piece of legislation." This otherwise gentle and dignified lady did not mince her words: "We're not paying attention to politicians any more. They don't have the guts to come out and say bilingual education programs don't work."[31]

A MEETING IN GLENDALE

In early February 1999, about thirty Hispanic parents and students gathered for a meeting in cochair Norma Alvarez's refurbished garage in Glendale. Two high school students who had learned English through immersion explained how much better off they were than their friends who had remained in bilingual classes and still could not speak or write decent English.

Parents talked about having moved from their neighborhoods to escape schools that had forced their children into bilingual education. Some wanted to take up residence where their children could attend schools in the Alhambra Elementary School District in west Phoenix; Latinos enrolled in those schools were making impressive academic gains through immersion methods. Unfortunately, the demand for homes in that area exceeded availability.

Alvarez expressed bewilderment that Joe Eddie Lopez had become the leading opponent of the initiative. She had known the senator and his wife for about thirty years, and she recalled not only Rosie's help with her son Jeff but also that the Lopezes had insisted on having their own son removed from a bilingual class at a junior high school in southwest Phoenix about twenty years prior.

The others in the room shook their heads and opined that the senator was being pressured by the bilingual education lobby "that nearly swallowed up his own son."[32] While this conversation was going on, Navarrette, a guest at the meeting, was taking notes for a column that appeared a few days later under the headline "Sen. Lopez's Stance on Bilingual Education a Mystery."

ISSUES ARE DEBATED IN PUBLIC FORUMS

Both the proponents and the opponents of the initiative spent hours preparing and participating in debates that were set up at town halls, community centers, colleges, and television stations throughout the state. The proponents were usually cochairs Margaret Garcia Dugan and Hector Ayala, appearing either individually or together as a team.

Senator Joe Eddie Lopez and Sal Gabaldón, chair of the English Department at TUSD's Pueblo Magnet High School, were the main debaters on the other side. Occasionally they drew upon a pool of articulate school administrators and professors of education to help.

Many attendees at these debates were affiliated with bilingual education through their jobs. Occasionally non-Hispanic parents showed up. Their children were learning Spanish in classes that offered both English and Spanish to both their children and the Hispanic LEP students, although funding of these dual-language programs relied on money designated solely for the education of the LEP children.

The Latino parents of the actual LEP students did not show up, except in small numbers on rare occasions. Sometimes Hispanic teenagers who felt bilingual education had either served them well or hindered their academic progress came to speak.

There was evidence that it was not just the parents Ayala had canvassed who supported immersion over bilingual education. Data from *A Lot to Be Thankful For*, a national study completed in 1998 by Public Agenda, showed that 66 percent of Hispanic parents preferred their children to be taught English as quickly as possible, even if it meant they would fall behind in other subjects. An earlier survey of six hundred Hispanic parents found that more than 80 percent wanted their children taught in English and not in

Spanish, with 63 percent wanting them to learn English as quickly as possible.[33]

At some forums, especially as the campaign advanced, Dugan and Ayala were booed before they had begun to speak; a few minutes later, Lopez, Galbadón, and other initiative opponents received enthusiastic applause. Other times, the host and audience were quite polite and interested in the issues. The televised debates were particularly helpful in that a wide audience could be reached.

On March 20, 1999, Delores Tropiano interviewed Navarrette for the television program *The Phoenix File* on KUTP. Navarrette made it clear that he would like to see bilingual education improved but that the bilingual education establishment refused to allow standards, accountability, parental control, or limitations on children's time in the program.

On the second part of the show, Tropiano hosted a debate that pitted two elementary school administrators, Kent Scribner and Dan Wegener, against Ayala and Dugan.

Scribner, director of multilingual and cultural curriculum at the Roosevelt Elementary School District (RESD) in Phoenix, explained that bilingual education was academically sound because the learning of core subjects was not delayed while the LEP students gained fluency in English. He insisted that he would not support bilingual education if it were not good for mastering English.

When Ayala explained that parents had told him their children were sequestered in either a separate classroom or a separate area in the same classroom where they learned in Spanish, Scribner replied, "That sounds like a very poor bilingual program," calling it "de facto segregation." His positive attitude gave the impression that he had made sure the bilingual education program in his district worked well.

Unfortunately, the SAT-9 results for Scribner's district, where the student population was about 73 percent Hispanic and nearly four thousand of them were identified as LEP, told quite a different story. The average scores of all children in that district ranged from the 23rd to 29th percentiles in grades 3 through 8 in 1998.[34] In contrast, Alhambra Elementary School District, where many Hispanic parents wanted to move because of the schools, had an enrollment that same year that was 61 percent Hispanic, with more than six thousand of them LEP and all immersed in English. The Alhambra students' average scores on the SAT-9 ranged from the 49th to the 58th percentile in grades 3 through 8.[35] This corresponded to the national average, which is set at the 50th percentile.

Wegener, director of bilingual education in the Avondale Elementary School District, expounded upon the merits of bilingualism, stating that it was considered a hallmark of education throughout the world. Dugan countered that the *bi* in *bilingual education* was a misnomer because the students remained monolingual after being taught in Spanish for five or six years. Citing recent research on the brain, she elaborated that learning a second language was most effective when it occured between the ages of zero and ten.

Wegener praised his district's dual-language program, which he mentioned was popular with the parents in his district—however, he did not specify whether it was the English-speaking parents or the parents of the LEP students who favored it. About 59 percent of Avondale students were Hispanic, with more than one thousand of them LEP. The Avondale students' average scores on the SAT-9 ranged from the 33rd to the 44th percentiles in grades 3 through 8.[36] —better than the Roosevelt students but worse than the Alhambra ones.

ALHAMBRA'S SUCCESSFUL IMMERSION PROGRAM

It would seem that more Arizona elementary schools, especially those with high numbers of LEP students, would have chosen to model their LEP programs after Alhambra's. However, doing so would have forced them to forfeit millions of dollars in federal funds.

Alhambra Elementary superintendent Carol Peck had not taken the federal funds that were tied to bilingual education. Instead, she had been able to fund her district's many programs for at-risk students through 130 partnerships with businesses and community groups.[37] The low-income citizens in her district voted for an increase in their local taxes so the district could provide pre-kindergarten and all-day kindergarten classes, making it possible for many LEP students to reach English proficiency before entering first grade.

The teachers in Alahambra were trained to teach reading using a phonics program that was chosen by the teachers at each school. In addition, the Alhambra schools offered Spanish lessons based on the vocabulary of a particular class for fifteen minutes each day, allowing English-dominant children the opportunity to develop basic Spanish skills with their LEP peers.

POSITIVE RESPONSES

After California's English proficiency test scores were released in early May 2000, the national media expressed praise for the success of the initiative in that state. The *Los Angeles Daily News*, the *Orange County Register*, the *Richmond Times Dispatch*, and the *Washington Times* reported that the reclassification rate to FEP had increased from 8 percent in the last year of bilingual education to over 10 percent two years after California Prop 227 was passed. The articles attributed the success to Prop 227 and common sense.

Michael Barone of *US News & World Report* was impressed by the improvement of LEP children in the Oceanside Unified School District in California, where the initiative had been strictly enforced. Barone visited one of that district's second grade classrooms.

In a commentary, Barone chided the teachers' union and politicians for having looked the other way in spite of the obvious failure of bilingual education:

> Latino politicians and foundation-funded activist groups gave loud public support to it while often admitting privately that it wasn't working. Education schools spun theories of how kids would learn English better by learning in Spanish, and teachers' unions pocketed dues from "bilingual" teachers who got $5,000 bonuses. Democrats reflexively voted for it, and Republicans paid it no heed: It wasn't their kids. [38]

ENDORSEMENT FROM A US CONGRESSMAN

On June 5, 2000, US Representative Matt Salmon of Arizona gave a press conference in Phoenix to endorse the new initiative. He was joined by Oceanside Unified School District superintendent Ken Noonan, the four leaders of English for the Children—Arizona, national chairman Ron Unz, and about seventy-five others.

Salmon stated that bilingual education had failed in its mission to teach children English and had denied thousands of young Americans the opportunity to fully realize the American dream. He attempted to defuse any effort to paint him as a racist: "There are a lot of people that are going to come forward tomorrow and say Matt Salmon is a racist. All I can say is the results in California have been phenomenal." [39]

OFFICIALLY PROPOSITION 203

On Tuesday, June 27, 2000, the officials of English for the Children—Arizona, Unz, and about fifty supporters submitted several boxes of petitions to the Arizona Secretary of State at the Arizona State Capitol in Phoenix. They had amassed about 165,000 signatures, an amount that far exceeded the required 101,762 signatures.

When *Arizona Republic* reporter Daniel Gonzalez stopped Unz to ask him about the financing of the initiative, he answered frankly that he had contributed $100,000 to the campaign. [40] Most of the money was used to pay the petitioners who had collected the required signatures, a practice commonly employed by anyone seeking political office or change through the initiative process in Arizona, but frowned upon by the press.

After Unz talked to the reporter about the superiority of immersion education, John Petrovic, bilingual education researcher at Arizona State University (ASU), told the reporter that Unz's assertion was "a lie." He insisted that bilingual education students had consistently scored higher on standardized tests, adding that a majority of Arizona's LEP students were in English immersion programs.[41] He asked, "This experiment in California has been a dismal failure, so why should we think that it is going to do any better here?"[42]

Petrovic was correct to say that the majority of LEP children in Arizona were not officially in bilingual programs. However, his claim that the bilingual education students had outperformed the others was questionable and was probably based on faulty data from the Arizona Department of Education (see pp. 26–27).

Within two months, Petrovic's argument would backfire. The 2000 California SAT-9 results would show that the 1.4 million LEP children in that state had made gains beyond expectations. Meanwhile, the signatures on the Arizona petitions were found sufficient to put the initiative on the ballot—known officially now as Proposition 203.

CALIFORNIA'S SUCCESS HELPS ARIZONA'S CAUSE

The Arizona initiative gained support when the *New York Times* celebrated the SAT-9 gains of the LEP children on Sunday, August 20, 2000, with a front-page article. It revealed that the reading scores of second grade LEP children had increased from the 19th to the 28th percentile in national rankings, and in mathematics scores had increased from the 27th to the 41st percentile.

The article further elaborated that it was too early to know how much the rise in scores was due to the erasure of bilingual education and how much was because class sizes in the second grade had been reduced as well. Nevertheless, the outcome was noteworthy because it put the lie to bilingual education proponents' predictions that the Spanish-speaking students' scores would plummet.[43]

The article focused on Oceanside superintendent Ken Noonan, noting that for the first time Oceanside had outscored the neighboring Vista Unified School District, where about half of the LEP students had been able to continue in bilingual education due to parental pressure and the use of waivers.

The *Wall Street Journal* told a similar story about the Oceanside and Vista school districts, with praise for Ron Unz: "Neither political party had the nerve to challenge either the special interests—especially the entrenched teachers—of the bilingual lobby or Latino politicians who played the race card. Then in 1998, software entrepreneur Ron Unz put a citizen initiative on the ballot to stop the insanity."[44]

Eight days after the *New York Times* article appeared, *USA Today* ran the editorial "Bilingual Education Fails Test, Exposing Deeper Problem." It accused the education establishment of poor research: "If the trend continues, as appears likely, it would suggest hundreds of thousands of children in California and elsewhere were hobbled by flawed bilingual programs."[45]

On September 21, 2000, State Representative Laura Knaperek endorsed Prop 203. She stated that the California test scores had convinced her, and went on to say, "Our best hope for providing these children with a decent education is by supporting Proposition 203, dismantling bilingual education, and relying on programs which work."[46]

According to Don Soifer, vice president of the Lexington Institute, bilingual education lost support from members of both major political parties because of California's 2000 SAT-9 results. Soifer elaborated that Santa Ana school board member Rosemarie Avila blamed her district's marginal growth in scores on failing to get rid of bilingual education. Moreover, Governor Gray Davis, formerly against the initiative, now praised the test score increases as "important gains."

Figure 3.1, compiled by Soifer, shows a comparison of the nationally normed SAT-9 results for LEP students in major California school districts. [*Note:* San José continued its bilingual education programs due to a prior agreement with federal authorities.] The numbers are percentile rank scores, with 50 being the average national percentile rank score.

Long-term Trend in Reading

School District	2000 Reading	1999 Reading	1998 Reading	Total Change	2000 Math	1999 Math	1998 Math	Total Change
Oceanside SD	23.2	17.8	12.0	+ 11.2	37.2	27.2	18.6	+ 18.6
Santa Barbara SD	27.0	21.2	16.4	+ 10.6	39.0	31.8	23.2	+ 15.8
Los Angeles USD	17.2	14.6	13.4	+ 3.8	27.0	24.0	20.8	+ 6.2
San Jose SD	16.6	15.6	15.0	+ 1.6	28.6	23.4	20.0	+8.6
Statewide LEP	21.0	18.4	15.6	+ 5.4	33.8	28.6	23.6	+10.2
Statewide All Students	45.6	42.2	39.6	+ 6.0	54.8	48.0	42.6	+12.2

Figure 3.1. Long-Term Trend in Reading

Soifer explained that other changes at Oceanside, besides the elimination of bilingual education, had most likely contributed to the dramatic rise in scores. The school day had been extended by an hour, a phonics-based language arts program had been implemented, and a zero-tolerance for violence policy had been put into effect.[47]

Bilingual education advocate Professor Stephen Krashen insisted on numerous occasions that the overall increase in California LEP achievement scores was because the SAT-9 was new to California students and an emphasis had been put on test preparation. He cited research that showed that "after new tests are introduced, test scores rise." Some test-taking skills could have raised scores without an increase in competence, and "even if we accept the SAT-9 scores as valid, there is no evidence linking test score increases to dropping bilingual education."[48]

Krashen was right to scrutinize the data that the media believed favored immersion over bilingual education; however, his credibility was in doubt because he had not assessed bilingual education programs with the same meticulousness.

With so much of the national press favoring California Prop 227, the polls showed that 70 to 74 percent of the Arizona voters favored the initiative in the two to three months preceding the election. Consequently, bilingual education advocates resorted to desperate measures: They filed a lawsuit against the initiative. This resulted in a slight change in its wording but did not eliminate it. They also sent their supporters to reservations in an attempt to scare Native American parents into thinking their native language programs were at risk.

NATIVE AMERICANS RALLY

Several hundred members of the Navajo, Hopi, Salt River, and other tribes rallied against Prop 203 at the Arizona State Capitol in Phoenix on Friday, October 13, 2000. Some of the elderly members of the Navajo Nation who had served as Code Talkers during World War II carried signs at the rally to remind people of their role in winning the war.

State Senator Jack Jackson of Window Rock said that he could not remember a larger Native American protest at the State Capitol since his election sixteen years earlier. According to another official, about nineteen Navajo children classified as LEP could be affected by the initiative along with many more belonging to other tribes.

Ron Unz had explained in an *Arizona Republic* letter to the editor on September 8 that a legal opinion regarding the almost identical proposition in California stated that the initiative would not affect the Native Americans' educational programs. However, according to Andrew Andreoli, who oversaw Native American education for the California Department of Education, the California initiative had had no effect on native language programs in that state because the issue had not been challenged in court. [49] Because few Native Americans in California spoke their native language, there had not been the need for bilingual programs on reservations.

When asked about the controversy, a spokesman for Arizona Attorney General Janet Napolitano said that it was not the attorney general's policy to give a legal opinion on an initiative before an election. [50] Three months after Prop 203 passed, on February 15, 2001, Napolitano informed the tribes that "Proposition 203 cannot prohibit a State public school located on the Reservation or elsewhere from teaching students Native American language and culture." She further noted that these classes may be offered whether or not the children were already proficient in English. [51]

Had Napolitano presented a legal opinion on this matter a few months earlier, she could have saved Native Americans $85,000—the amount they had contributed to Arizona Citizens Opposed to Proposition 203. Interestingly, two years later, in 2002, Napolitano would defeat former Congressman Matt Salmon for the position of governor of Arizona because of the overwhelming support she received from the Native Americans.

THE LEAD-UP TO ELECTION DAY

Although generally supportive of bilingual education, *Arizona Republic* writer Richard Ruelas accused the bilingual education supporters of having "decided to play politics" using a commercial that was running ten times a day on five of the Phoenix Area's top-rated radio stations. The commercial pushed "parental choice" and did not even mention bilingual education, using terms such as *outsiders* and *hidden agendas* to appeal to listeners. Ruelas found it especially ironic that major funding for the ad came from gambling casino profits—that is, mostly Native Americans in the Salt River Community. [52]

Through the month of October, there were rallies—mostly in opposition to Prop 203—and highly contentious debates. People held up signs—"Bilingualism instead of Ethnocentrism" and the common "Ron Unz, go home!"—at various functions. Several times, opponents to the initiative stated that the measure was a threat to deaf children learning sign language, although, as Margaret Garcia Dugan frequently pointed out, the measure exempted children with special needs.

At the last debate, which took place on October 26, 2000, at Arizona State University, the debaters were met by students from Movimiento Estudiantil Chicano de Aztlán (MECHA), who wore T-shirts that read, "Ask me why I'm fasting." Others were carrying signs with the slogans: "No on Prop 203,"

"Takes Away Parental Choice," and "My Money My Choice." Once in the hall, the students showed hostility toward the two speakers in favor of the initiative, Margaret Garcia Dugan and Ron Unz, booing them loudly.

Dugan looked directly at a student before beginning her speech and said, "Young man who is flipping me the bird, I do not believe that I would do that to another person. This is my opinion, this is my practice, and this is my life. I am not here saying this because I have a vested interest in it. My life will continue whether this proposition passes or not."[53] The room suddenly quieted down, and Dugan later received polite applause.

According to Unz, the polls continued to show an easy win for the initiative. However, throughout the weekend before the election, various groups ran ads on TV and radio claiming that LEP children enrolled in bilingual education had shown greater academic achievement than those in ESL, according to ADE data. The Proposition 203 proponents ran no ads.

VICTORY

On the night of Tuesday, November 7, 2000, Proposition 203 won by a large margin, later computed to equal 63 percent of the vote. Margaret Garcia Dugan stated to the media, "I am very happy that Arizona voters have given us the compassionate vote to help our children be proficient in English so they can pursue their dreams in this country."[54]

The triumphant, beaming leaders and supporters of Prop 203 clapped loudly after state superintendent Lisa Graham Keegan vowed to the media that she would respect the will of the people and make sure the new law was enforced in the schools.

The following day, State Senator Joe Eddie Lopez threatened a court challenge: "Besides being bad public policy, it is a very poorly crafted instrument, so there definitely will be some legal challenge to six or seven different aspects of it." He admitted, however, that it would be difficult because legal action against the similar California law had failed.[55]

According to the Arizona Secretary of State's records on campaign expenditures, anti–Proposition 203 groups had spent $348,848 altogether. Of that amount, $85,000 had come from Native American tribes and $85,150 from the teachers' unions. English for the Children—Arizona had spent $229,789, with Ron Unz contributing $186,886—81 percent of the total.

Chapter Four

Closing the "Loopholes"

The landslide victory in Arizona on November 7, 2000, encouraged people in other states to consider creating similar ballot initiatives. A Spanish-language radio talk show host in Dallas, Texas, who had interviewed Proposition 203 Chair Maria Mendoza on Election Day said that her program was flooded with calls from people who agreed that bilingual education was a failure. The talk show host explained, "What I heard from listeners is people want their children to learn English as quickly as possible."[1]

Indeed, the back-to-back wins in California and Arizona had made an impact nationally and would soon be followed by ballot measures in Colorado and Massachusetts. Unfortunately, enthusiasm was sadly lacking among educators and politicians in the state that had most recently passed its anti–bilingual education initiative.

FAILURE TO ENFORCE PROPOSITION 203

The day after the election, school board president Robert Zamora of the Isaac Elementary School District in southwest Pheonix urged other Arizona districts to continue offering bilingual education in spite of the new law. He added that he was talking to lawyers to weigh the ramifications of ignoring the initiative before asking his school district's board members to adopt a proposal that would officially defy it.[2]

The board president would soon discover that a formal action opposing the law was unnecessary, because bilingual education would continue in Arizona schools pretty much the same as it had been before the election. Politicians and bilingual education proponents would circumvent Proposition 203 by interpreting its provisions guilefully and then calling them "loopholes." Amazingly, not a single government official would question this transgression.

Ultimately, the English for the Children proposition would prevail, but only after another long, hard-fought political campaign.

THE LAW IS UNDERMINED

Arizona superintendent of public instruction Lisa Graham Keegan talked about the new law before the Scottsdale Parent Council on January 9, 2001, two months after the election. In a front-page *Arizona Republic* article, Keegan was quoted as saying that she would allow Arizona schools to continue bilingual education "as long as students are learning English and making academic progress." According to Keegan, "Bilingual programs are successful when kids are speaking two languages, and their academics are on par. Do what you want and make it work, and nobody is going to go ballistic."[3]

Scottsdale superintendent of schools Barbara Erwin appeared confused after listening to Keegan at the council meeting. Erwin interpreted Keegan's words to mean that bilingual education could continue as long as it was successful.[4]

According to Keegan, "The way we'll know if they're not following 203 is if the kids are making zero progress. Then yes, we'll talk to the school." She added that the provision of Proposition 203 to test limited English proficient students annually on their English skills would be followed and that would determine what was working.[5]

Ron Unz responded immediately to Keegan's statements, "She is indicating by her quotes that she is above the law, that she, rather than the people of Arizona, can decide the law."[6]

State Senator Joe Eddie Lopez found Keegan's approach to be "most practical." However, he warned that anyone who interpreted Keegan's comments "as providing the freedom to continue teaching in a child's home language, most often Spanish, could open themselves up to lawsuits under the new law."[7]

Unz expressed amazement that Lopez, the leader of the anti–Proposition 203 campaign, was warning the bilingual advocates about penalties they would face if they disobeyed the law.[8]

Proposition 203 cochair Norma Alvarez insisted, "If there's a law, we have to enforce it. If not, our work has been for nothing."[9]

The day after the controversial front-page article appeared, Keegan attempted to clarify her point of view, asserting, "Of course I'm going to enforce the proposition. But I've never interpreted the initiative as English-only. . . . Specific details, such as the amount of time that can be spent in other language instruction or what penalties can or will be enforced for noncompliance, are being worked out."[10]

Keegan's vow on election night to respect the will of the people and enforce Proposition 203 was now in doubt. She had emboldened its opponents.

THE "TOO FEW TESTS" PROBLEM

Prop 203 eliminated the exemption that excused English language learners from taking a standardized test in English for three consecutive years, mandating the schools administer yearly "a standardized, nationally-normed written test of academic subject matter" to all Arizona public school students grades 2 and higher.[11] Thus, the English for the Children leaders were correct to expect the Arizona Department of Education to give the state-designated SAT-9 in the spring of 2001 to LEP students (now called English language learners).

This was especially important to Prop 203 cochair Margaret Garcia Dugan, who hoped that the test results could be used to establish baseline data from which the achievement of ELLs could be measured accurately after Prop 203 was implemented. But surprisingly, ADE authorities said that they could not administer the test to everyone because they had not ordered enough test booklets. In its place, the Aprenda, a Spanish version of the Arizona Instrument to Measure Standards, would be given again to third, fifth and eighth grade ELLs in bilingual classes.

"A WORKING KNOWLEDGE OF ENGLISH"

Proposition 203 opponent Sal Gabaldón explained in a column for the *Arizona Daily Star* that one provision of the law actually required bilingual education. He quoted the initiative that "any school in which 20 or more students receive waivers for bilingual education must provide bilingual education." Gabaldón elaborated further that students eligible for a waiver would include "all students who are under 10 years of age and have a working knowledge of English."[12]

In e-mail correspondence Lopez elaborated further, "The law does not specify how an oral evaluation should be conducted or what scores to use. In fact, the law would appear to allow a teacher to determine from a simple conversation with an English learner that he or she already knew enough English to qualify for a waiver."[13]

Both Gabaldón and Lopez were omitting an important detail: Whether measured by oral evaluation or by a standardized test, the child would have to score "approximately at or above the state average for his grade level or at or above the 5th grade average, whichever was lower," to qualify for that waiver.[14] Thus an oral evaluation would suffice, but it would have to be equal in difficulty and depth to a standardized test of English vocabulary comprehension, reading, and writing at the specified grade level.

TWO-WEEK SUMMER PROGRAMS

Many school districts such as Glendale Elementary, Creighton Elementary, and Tucson Unified accepted Lopez's questionable interpretation of the provision as accurate, but decided it best to provide official documentation. Thus, the teachers set up two-week intense summer programs during which they were able to bring ELLs who knew little or no English to a very basic level of oral competence. As proof of this amazing feat, the teachers administered the oral section of an English language proficiency test to the students, and virtually all of them passed. According to the teachers, this qualified the ELLs for the waiver that exempts "children who already know English."[15]

There were some serious problems with this process:

- The teachers had access to the specific items on the test, so the test results lacked validity.
- The test was so short that it was easy for the teachers to prepare the children to give the correct responses even if the children didn't understand much of the language.
- The level designated "pass" was still "limited English," and so did not meet the oral language proficiency standard of Proposition 203.

The teachers, with help from Lopez, had indeed put together a scheme to save bilingual education.

PARENTS ARE ENCOURAGED TO SIGN WAIVERS

For the next several months, English for the Children officials Maria Mendoza, Hector Ayala, Margaret Garcia Dugan, and Norma Alvarez heard reports from school employees that parents were being coerced in various ways:

- Schools were putting on social events such as barbecues for the parents of ELLs to coax the parents into applying for waivers.
- Parents were being warned of possible deportation if they refused to sign waivers.
- An employee of a large high school district was calling parents of Spanish-speaking children to promise honors credits to the children who enrolled in bilingual classes.

Cochair Hector Ayala lamented, "What it tells me is that we were all exactly right when we said the bilingual education establishment won't go away very easily. . . . I suspect that 95 percent of the people signing waivers are not coming forward of their own accord. I believe they are being recruited."[16]

A year later, a teacher of ELLs at an elementary school in west Phoenix explained to a newspaper reporter the system they were using at her school: "We waiver all the kids in. We have to explain everything in Spanish and convince the parents to sign the waivers." In addition, the school had created a form letter that allowed parents to fill in certain blanks to make it specific to their child.[17]

Segments on local news programs occasionally featured ELL classes conducted in Spanish, giving the explanation that the schools could continue bilingual education because of the Prop 203 "loopholes."

SUPERINTENDENT KEEGAN'S RESIGNATION AND REPLACEMENT

Superintendent of Public Instruction Lisa Graham Keegan resigned quite unexpectedly in May 2001 to head the Education Leaders Council in Washington, DC. Shortly thereafter, Governor Jane Hull appointed thirty-three-year-old Jaime Molera, Hull's top education adviser, to Keegan's former position.

Molera did not approve of Proposition 203. In the fall of 2001, after having been in office for about four months, he expressed his opinion in an interview that appeared in the *AEA Advocate*, a publication of the Arizona Education Association (AEA), the largest teachers' union in Arizona:

> In my opinion, Proposition 203 was a big mistake. It's throwing the baby out with the bath water. It's true that major reforms were needed in bilingual education when kids aren't mastering English after a certain number of years. But we had two polarized camps. One said, "Do absolutely nothing." The other said, "Destroy the system." That side had a lot of money. So they won.[18]

Molera sent out a guidance pamphlet, but it was not helpful for anyone serious about implementing the new law. It offered excerpts from the actual initiative but lacked interpretation that could clarify the changes the schools needed to make. The schools were expected to figure it out themselves, with the implication that whatever they decided to do regarding Prop 203 would be acceptable to the ADE.

A new election in which the citizens of Arizona would be voting for the top state officials—including Arizona's superintendent of public instruction—was scheduled for November 5, 2002. Molera, was considered a shoo-in to win the Republican primary for this office, mostly because no Republican incumbent holding high office in Arizona had ever been defeated in a primary. Molera would then compete in the general election against one of the Democratic candidates, who, like Molera, supported bilingual education.

NO ASSISTANCE FROM LEGISLATORS

Occasionally, during the summer and fall of 2001, the state legislature scheduled hearings that dealt with Prop 203. It soon became obvious to anyone who attended that the legislators and their aides intended to do as little as possible to enforce this law. For example, they agreed among themselves that Prop 203 permitted the placement of even beginning ELLs with regular students in the mainstream, rather than in their own separate classroom. This contradicted what was actually written in the law:

> Local schools shall be encouraged to mix together in the same classroom English learners from different native-language groups but with the same degree of English fluency. Once English learners have acquired a good working knowledge of English and are able to do regular school work in English, they shall no longer be classified as English learners and shall be transferred to English language mainstream classrooms. [19]

When Margaret Garcia Dugan occasionally showed up at meetings, her points of view and concerns were politely dismissed. It didn't appear to matter to the legislators that Dugan, the principal of Glendale High School, a "minority-majority" high school that the ADE had designated as having a "model structured English immersion ELL program"—had helped write Prop 203.

On July 24, 2001, Sal Gabaldón and Leonardo Basurto of the Tucson Unified School District addressed an Arizona House and Senate working group, of which Senator Joe Eddie Lopez was a member. The implementation of Prop 203 was a major focus of the bipartisan group. Gabaldón and Basurto explained how their district was supposedly enforcing Prop 203 and recommended that the results of bilingual education and English immersion programs be compared before the official implementation of the law in the fall. [20]

No one was there to explain the discrepancies regarding the state achievement test results that had made such a comparison impossible (see chap. 3, pp. 26–27). State Representative Linda Gray, head of the group and chairperson of the House Education Committee, turned the subject back to student achievement: "My concern is, what are the most effective programs so that we are not leaving students behind . . . at the 30th percentile." [21]

After attending one of the legislative meetings, *Arizona Republic* colum-nist Robert Robb, who had recommended voting against Proposition 203, remarked in his September 9, 2001, column, "In the last election the people of Arizona decreed that a particular method of instructing English learners, immersion, be used in our public schools. Instead of implementing the will of the voters in good faith, school districts around the state are scrambling to circumvent it."[22]

THE ARIZONA DEPARTMENT OF EDUCATION COST STUDY

The legislators should have taken the time to read the ADE English Acquisi-tion Cost Study that had been completed by the Institute for Research in English Acquisition and Development and a reputable accounting group from California in May 2001. This study offered details about the Arizona school districts' ELL programs and showed achievement rising as schools moved from bilingual to English immersion instruction (see chap. 5, p. 65).[23]

The cost study consultants were scheduled to come before the legislature to answer questions and offer suggestions. However, the meeting was can-celed after Keegan's resignation and the $213,000 cost study was then disregarded.

POLITICIANS SHUN PROP 203 LEADERS

US Representative Matt Salmon, who had endorsed Prop 203 in 2000, was now vying for the Republican gubernatorial nomination, with the hope of winning the 2002 election. In 1999, Salmon and House Education Committee chairman Rep. Bill Goodling had sponsored House Representative 2 (HR 2), legislation to be added to the Elementary and Secondary Education Act of 2000 that would require consent from parents of ELLs before putting their children in a program and eliminate the provision that required at least 75 percent of ELL grant money be spent on bilingual programs.

Thus, Hector Ayala had testified on behalf of HR 2, at Salmon's request, at a House subcommittee meeting in 1999.[24] Whereas HR 2 passed eventual-ly in the House, it failed in the Senate; however, the provisions of the bill were implemented in 2001 as part of the No Child Left Behind Act (NCLB).

Ayala called Salmon several times in 2001 and 2002. It seemed likely that Salmon would be open to making sure Prop 203 was implemented, but Salmon did not respond to any communication from Ayala in spite of their earlier friendly relationship. It was later reported that Salmon did not want to appear critical of Molera in any way and had been advised by his political consultant to stay clear of English for the Children representatives. As the race played out, Salmon would likely have defeated Democrat Janet Napolitano for the Arizona governorship had he supported their cause, as he had done previously.

Molera himself continued to give the Prop 203 group the cold shoulder, avoiding their several requests for a meeting with him. This was an error on Molera's part, because the group's leaders—Mendoza, Ayala, Dugan, and Alvarez—had been pleased with his appointment to the position of Arizona superintendent of public instruction. Had he merely met with the group and assured them that he was doing what he could, it is likely they would have believed him and not interfered with his campaign to win the 2002 election to his appointed office.

The group assumed that Molera, a conservative Hispanic from Nogales, Arizona, surely agreed with the people of Nogales, who had voted overwhelmingly for Prop 203. In fact, the people of Nogales had ended bilingual education and implemented SEI in their schools even *before* the initiative passed, out of disgust that their predominantly Hispanic young people had not gained proficiency in English after attending Nogales schools for a full thirteen years.

Unfortunately, Salmon and Molera had not lived up to the group's expectations, and the demise of Proposition 203 appeared inevitable.

A CHAMPION OF ENGLISH FOR THE CHILDREN EMERGES

Finally, after months of one disappointment after another, Ron Unz and the Arizona leadership of English for the Children found a champion for their cause in attorney and former state legislator Tom Horne, a candidate in the Republican primary against Jaime Molera for the office of state superintendent. As president of the governing board of the very large Paradise Valley Unified School District, located in north Phoenix and north Scottsdale, Horne was credited with having raised academic achievement, cut administrative costs, and brought discipline to that district.

On Monday, March 18, 2002, Horne announced officially his candidacy. He was described by the *Arizona Republic* as coming out "swinging" with criticisms that Molera would water down the state's high school graduation exam and was not enforcing Prop 203.[25]

In response, Molera's spokesman, Tom Collins, accused Horne of missing the facts. Moreover, Collins "castigated Horne for unnecessarily injecting race into the campaign."[26] Collins asked, "Is the assumption that because Superintendent Molera is Hispanic . . . he won't enforce the law [replacing bilingual education with English immersion]? He is implementing the law. I don't know what the basis for all this is."[27]

In a press release dated March 20, Horne responded that Collins's accusation was outrageous. He said, "Molera's opposition to the referendum replacing bilingual education with English immersion is well documented, and his failure to enforce the law even though it was overwhelmingly passed by the voters is also well documented."

Horne continued, "This criticism has nothing whatsoever to do with Molera's race. The public is fed up with the technique by which someone, who is unable to deal with the substance of a legitimate disagreement, instead plays the race card. This technique has been overdone, and people are wise to it."[28]

TOM HORNE GAINS SUPPORT

On Tuesday, July 16, Horne received a formal endorsement from the Arizona English for the Children leaders at a press conference, where Maria Mendoza said,

> Although Arizona voters passed Proposition 203, dismantling bilingual education, by nearly a 2-to-1 margin in November 2000, news reports have indicated that thousands of Hispanic students still remain in bilingual education classes throughout Arizona. Most of these students have been placed in Spanish-language classes after their school districts declare them to have a good knowledge of English. Proposition 203 leaders have repeatedly declared this waiver procedure an illegal fraud and have bitterly denounced it for most of the last year. Tom Horne, a Harvard-educated attorney and long-time school board official, has made full enforcement of Proposition 203 one of the centerpieces of his campaign against Mr. Molera in the Republican Primary.[29]

Horne went from mostly unknown to favored candidate of Republican voters within a few months. He put two effective ads on television that stated his vision and ridiculed Molera for his plan to allow students to substitute projects for passing the mandatory high school AIMS. He continued to hammer away at Molera's unwillingness to enforce Prop 203, a point that Molera could not defend.

MOLERA'S CAMPAIGN LOSES GROUND

Horne was spending more than $500,000 of his own money on the primary contest. This put Molera at a disadvantage because, as a publicly funded Clean Elections candidate, he was outspent by nearly 5 to 1. Consequently, Molera showed desperation and angered many Religious Right Republicans by appearing for about thirty seconds in a television ad endorsing a ballot proposition in support of gambling, paid for by Native American tribes.

Molera also made the foolish mistake of not submitting a picture and a statement to the candidates' statement pamphlet that the Citizens Clean Election Commission sent to every registered voter. Thus he missed out on an opportunity early in his campaign to sell himself in a way that would have cost him nothing.

Molera was late in supporting vouchers—probably because he had avoided the subject in order to secure the support of the teachers' unions, which he lost nevertheless. On the other hand, Horne was clear about supporting charter schools and tax credits but not vouchers, explaining that the Arizona state constitution specifically outlawed them.

Molera also backed a Phoenix superintendent who attempted to ban Spanish from his schools' campuses during recess. In an attempt to appear in favor of Prop 203, Molera showed himself to be ignorant of the initiative, because anyone who had read it knew that it did not restrict students from speaking their native language on school grounds. As Penny Kotterman, president of the state's teachers' union, stated, "It harkens back to the days when children were punished for speaking Spanish on campus."[30] Prop 203 did not in any way mandate that LEP children speak only English, just that they be taught predominantly in English, not Spanish (with some exceptions allowed). Molera was wrong to support the school superintendent who tried to force children to speak English on the playground. Kotterman was referring back to a time in Arizona when Hispanic children were actually punished for speaking Spanish. Molera was trying to appear supportive of 203 that 63 percent of the voters had passed—but, instead, displayed publicly his own ignorance toward Prop 203.

2002 REPUBLICAN PRIMARY RESULTS

On September 10, 2002, Tom Horne beat Jaime Molera with 41.2 percent of the vote to Molera's 30.3 percent. A third candidate, Keith Bee, received 28.5 percent.

The following day, the *Arizona Republic* editorial board, which had supported Molera for the nomination, put forth in their newspaper a scathing response to Horne's victory:

> A close second on the disappointment scale [the first being Matt Salmon's big win as the Republican gubernatorial candidate] was the poor showing by Republican Superintendent of Public Instruction Jaime Molera. Perhaps this race was about money, which self-financed Tom Horne had in bucketsful. More darkly, it also raises questions about the willingness of Republicans to elect anyone but Anglos.[31]

Two days later on KAET's television show *Journalists Roundtable*, Mark Flatten, a writer for the *East Valley Tribune*, sparred with Keven Willey, editorial editor of the *Arizona Republic*, about her editorial board's remarks concerning Horne's win:

Mark Flatten: Well, really there are sort of two competing theories. . . . The first one goes like this, across the board, conservatives turned out in huge numbers. . . . Jaime was weak on AIMS. Jaime was weak on bilingual. Jaime never defined a big picture vision for education. And Tom Horne spent a lot of money. The second theory from the editorial board is Republicans are all racists. if you look at the numbers . . .

Keven Wiley: To portray this as the fact that the conservative Republicans won is ludicrous. Horne is a former Democrat. I don't think it was the partisan—what it was was the spending. I mean, he outspent 5 to 1. It's not just the act of spending, it's what you do with the money. What he did with the money was run a set of commercials that lays the race issue in a way that was unfair and reflected poorly on Jaime Molera and that's why he won.

Mark Flatten: No, what he ran on the race—the so-called race issue—was bilingual education, which was approved by a fairly substantial margin by Arizona voters. He convinced people that Jaime was not committed to it, that he was not enforcing it.

THE 2002 GENERAL ELECTION

Less than a week after the primary election, "Learning English," an in-depth study on bilingual education by Professor Joseph M. Guzman, appeared in the nonpartisan periodical *Education Next.* In his stump speech during the general election, Horne talked effectively about two of Guzman's revelations: (1) that Hispanic former ESL students had obtained three-quarters of a year more education than students from bilingual programs; and, (2) that former ESL students had entered high skill professional occupations at almost twice the rate of students educated through bilingual education (see introduction, p. xxvi).[32]

Horne held a very different point of view from Democratic nominee Jay Blanchard on how to improve education in Arizona. Blanchard said that he would enforce Prop 203 but allow parents to choose bilingual education. Blanchard opposed AIMS, while Horne promised to strengthen it. And whereas Blanchard claimed to support charter schools, he also wanted to require them to hire only certified teachers, something that would have put many charters out of business. Horne fully supported charter schools and intended to increase their numbers.

On November 5, 2002, Tom Horne was elected to the office of Arizona Superintendent of Public Instruction with support from 50 percent of Arizona voters; Democrat Jay Blanchard received 46 percent, and Libertarian John Zajac received 4 percent.

PROMISE KEPT

On December 17, 2002, Superintendent of Public Instruction–Elect Tom Horne announced his leadership team. He named Margaret Garcia Dugan as the new associate superintendent of academic support of the ADE, stating, "Her appointment should erase any uncertainties as to whether I will fulfill my campaign promise to enforce that initiative."[33]

On February 13, 2003, speaking at the low-income, mostly Hispanic, academically reputable Andalucia Middle School in the Alhambra Elementary School District, Horne announced new guidelines for the implementation of what were now called the Arizona English Language Immersion Laws. He stated that the first waiver "has been abused by school districts qualifying students whose test scores show that they have 'limited' English language skills, as defined by the publishers of the tests." He explained that students would be required to demonstrate "good English language skills"—that is, proficiency in English—to qualify for dual-language programs.[34] Should schools choose not to comply with the guidelines, they would face penalties that included loss of accreditation and funding.[35]

Horne's guidelines set the cutoff scores for English fluency at 4 out of 5 on the state-approved Language Assessment Scales, rather than at 3 out of 5, which many schools preferred, and at equivalent levels on the three other state-approved proficiency tests. A Tucson school superintendent said this act alone would have a major impact on the number of students who would qualify for bilingual education.[36]

Dugan agreed with the new cutoff scores, explaining that some schools had deemed students competent in English even though, according to the test publishers' definitions, their scores on English tests showed they still had limited proficiency. According to Dugan, "Now if you're fluent [in English] you can go into bilingual education, and not until."[37]

Raquel Rubio-Goldsmith, a community activist and lecturer in the Mexican-American Studies Department at the University of Arizona, disagreed strongly with the guidelines, saying, "When laws are passed that do not reflect social reality, it's difficult to enforce them properly. The waiver is the one safety valve to help a very bad situation. Anything that makes it more difficult to get a waiver is problematic."[38]

In border towns such as Nogales and Douglas, not a single parent had requested a waiver. According to a newspaper report, many parents along the border could speak little or no English themselves and viewed "learning the language well to be just as important as learning math, reading and the other subjects."[39]

An ADE spokesperson reported that the Tucson Unified School District had submitted 3,296 waiver requests, and the Sunnyside Unified School District (SUSD) in south Tucson, 1,400 waiver requests.[40] Proponents of Prop 203 suspected that the high number of waiver requests in Tucson was the result of coercion of parents by school officials who were bent on keeping their dual-language programs afloat.

According to Horne, complaints regarding the guidelines were not coming from Hispanic parents but instead from Anglo parents whose children were enrolled in those programs: "They want their kids to learn Spanish from the Latino kids. I can see their point. It is good for their children to be bilingual . . . but not at the expense of the Latino kids. They [Latino ELLs] need to be in an English immersion program."[41]

Fluent in three languages himself, Horne clarified that he recognized the value of speaking two languages, and for that reason had no problem with dual language instruction—"so long as students first meet tough English fluency standards at their grade level."[42]

Finally, after four years of spending most of their spare time campaigning on the issue, Maria Mendoza, Hector Ayala, Margaret Garcia Dugan, and Norma Alvarez were successful in dismantling bilingual education in Arizona. However, bigger challenges loomed on the horizon for Superintendent Tom Horne: ending a costly lawsuit against the state of Arizona and implementing SEI.

Chapter Five

From Political Impasse to the US Supreme Court

The State of Arizona dealt with the class action lawsuit *Flores et al. v. the State of Arizona et al.* for more than two decades. It was a case concerning the education of limited-English students that appeared to be resolved, but was not really—or not completely. It took up time in court, not to mention the hours of preparation necessary for court proceedings and the enormous, incalculable costs to Arizona taxpayers.

Flores charged the state with violating the Equal Educational Opportunities Act of 1974, which codified the US Supreme Court ruling in *Lau v. Nichols*, "requir[ing] that school districts provide LEP students with a program of instruction calculated to make them proficient in speaking, understanding, reading, and writing English so that they can achieve the same academic standards required of all other students."[1] As straightforward and worthwhile as this goal may seem, the two sides were not able to agree on what it takes to achieve it or how much it should cost.

THE *FLORES* RULING

On January 24, 2000, the *Flores* case seemed to have come to an end when US District Court Judge Alfredo Marquez ruled in favor of the plaintiffs. He charged the state with discrimination against limited English proficient students by not providing sufficient funding to educate them. [*Note*: The term *limited English proficient* was officially changed to *English language learner* in Arizona in 2001.]

Marquez determined that the Arizona legislature's funding of $150 yearly per LEP student was "arbitrary and capricious" because it was derived from a

1987 to 1988 estimate that had been neither updated nor adjusted for infla-
tion since that time. He accused the schools of placing students in over-
crowded classrooms with unqualified teachers and teachers' aides. Furthermore, he noted that the students were not provided with the tutoring or
instructional materials they needed.[2]

The case had originated in 1992 in Nogales, Arizona, a Mexican border
town of about twenty-two thousand inhabitants. Analizabeth Doan, a Nogales native who was at the time the bilingual education and curriculum
director for the Nogales Unified School District, worked with William Mor-
ris of the Arizona Justice Institute to help a group of parents file a class
action lawsuit against the Arizona Department of Education. Nogales parent
Miriam Flores and other parents claimed that their children were not learning
English well enough to participate academically in the school programs.

Eight years later, as a result of the January 2000 ruling, attorney Tim
Hogan of the Arizona Center for Law in the Public Interest had every reason
to believe that he had finally succeeded in winning the plaintiffs' case in
federal court. Lisa Graham Keegan, the state superintendent of public instruction, chose not to appeal the judge's decision. Six months later, she
entered into a consent decree with the plaintiffs. Hogan appeared to have
secured a great victory.

However, there was dissension over the outcome. State legislators were
infuriated and said they would not "kowtow to a federal judge." According to
Representative Eddie Farnsworth, "Essentially you have a federal judge trying to create statute from the bench. That's a violation of separation of
powers. I have no idea why Lisa Keegan signed the consent decree so fast.
The Legislature was excluded from all that."[3]

Hogan responded, "The Legislature is breaking a federal law, plain and
simple. They grumble about courts telling them what to do, but they won't do
things the right way. This is the state's main job: to educate kids."[4]

THE ARIZONA LEGISLATURE'S DILEMMA

The Arizona legislature faced a dilemma. Compliance with Marquez's consent order could require at least $45 million in additional yearly funding for
the state's LEP programs at a time when Arizona was facing a $1.5 billion
budget deficit. On the other hand, noncompliance could result in losing more
than $7 billion in federal funds.

The legislators feared that the voters' likely passage of Prop 203 in November 2000 would magnify the state's funding problem. Concerned that the
provisions of the *Flores* lawsuit would be incompatible with those of Prop
203, they dreaded the extent to which the state could be faced with additional
litigation and inestimable costs.[5]

COST STUDIES

In October 2000, Marquez ordered the state to conduct a cost study as an extension of the *Flores* consent decree. This undertaking would require thorough descriptions of the elements specific to LEP instruction in individual schools, along with their costs. Marquez originally ordered it to be completed by January 2001—an unrealistic time frame, especially in light of the upcoming election that could change LEP education completely.

That change happened on November 7, 2000, when the citizens of Arizona expressed their displeasure with bilingual education, approving Prop 203 with an overwhelming 63 percent of the vote. Subsequently, all parties of *Flores* would have to understand and deal with the implementation of sheltered English immersion (otherwise known as structured English immersion) instruction for Arizona's LEP students, as specified in the new law. Thus, after interviewing several interested parties, ADE officials chose for this project a nationally respected research organization that understood the particulars of SEI instruction, as well as a reputable organization familiar with school funding and audits.

On February 9, 2001, the ADE awarded contracts to two entirely separate entities: the Institute for Research in English Acquisition and Development in Washington, DC, to provide qualitative analyses of the SEI instruction and bilingual education programs chosen for the project; and Sjoberg Evashenk Consulting, LLC, in Sacramento, California,—which specialized in audits and evaluations of government programs—to identify and analyze the cost elements of those same programs.

Allowed fewer than three months to complete this project, both groups worked diligently, sometimes jointly but more often separately. They visited and analyzed the data of model SEI programs in six different schools (three of which were in Arizona), model bilingual education programs in two Phoenix schools, and English acquisition programs in each of the ten Nogales schools. The Sjoberg Evashenk consultants sent out surveys to hundreds of Arizona school districts requesting information about their schools' demographics, incremental costs for LEP services, funding, and achievement data.

On May 1, 2001, the two consulting groups submitted their combined results in a 345-page cost study, divided into four phases: (1) "The Costs of English Immersion in Six Model Programs" plus reviews of those programs; (2) "Statewide Incremental Costs and Resources Available to Fund English Acquisition Programs"; (3) "The Costs of a Model Bilingual Education Program" plus reviews of two such programs; and (4) "Incremental Costs and Resources Available to Fund English Acquisition Programs in the Nogales Unified School District" plus a review of the programs in each of the ten Nogales schools.

Neither group could come up with a specific per-student cost. READ officials reported that they had not been able to establish a correlation between student performance on standardized tests and the cost of implementing a program. Sjoberg Evashenk explained that the responses from 174 school districts and charter schools, out of 435 surveyed, had revealed no patterns or correlations between the proportions of LEP students in district/charter schools and the incremental costs of providing services to them. Moreover, their examiners had found no link between incremental per-student costs and the type of district or school, such as elementary, high school, unified, or charter. The costs per student ranged from zero to a high of $4,676.[6]

POLITICAL GRIDLOCK

Superintendent Lisa Graham Keegan scheduled a meeting with the legislature so the consultants from READ and Sjoberg Evashenk could discuss and answer questions about their findings. However, shortly after Keegan resigned on May 3, 2001, the meeting was canceled. It was not rescheduled. Considering other actions taking place during this post–Prop 203 election period (see chap. 4), and Jaime Molera's pro–bilingual education bent and opposition to Prop 203, the decision to drop this highly informative study was obviously political.

As part of their assignment, Dr. Rosalie Pedalino Porter, the director of READ, and Scott K. Baker, vice president of Eugene Research Institute in Eugene, Oregon, had spent a week interviewing officials and examining the school data in Nogales. They noted that the longer a school had provided SEI instruction, the higher the level of academic performance its students were achieving.[7] This particular aspect of the study should have motivated the legislators—or at least Molera, who had actually grown up in Nogales—to look further into what was going on in the Nogales schools. It did not.

The press reported that some legislators considered the cost study to have raised more questions than answers. State Senator Ruth Solomon, the head of the Senate Appropriations Committee, stated, "I'm very, very disappointed. This [the cost study] makes it worse than it was before."[8] Consequently, the ADE cost study was discarded.

Four years later, in February 2005, in compliance with new legislation and the original *Flores* consent order, the National Conference of State Legislatures (NCSL) presented a new cost study that recommended increases ranging from $670 to $2,571 per ELL. These amounts were based on responses from seven of the sixteen school districts the NCSL group had contacted.

Tim Hogan, the lawyer for the plaintiffs, found the NCSL study flawed "in one sense because it collected current ELL costs from too few school districts." He added, "The important part of the cost study is the exercise of figuring out what they should be spending, not what they are spending; we've already figured out from court that what they are spending is inadequate."[9]

Arizona Superintendent of Public Instruction Tom Horne stated, "The draft that they [the NCSL] came up with had no scientific basis and it was so bad that they actually wrote off their fee." He contended that an analysis of the techniques of the best-performing schools would be preferable.[10]

For more than five years after Marquez's ruling in 2000, the Arizona legislature had failed to create legislation the court would accept as compliant with the *Flores* consent order. Neither the 2001 ADE cost study nor the more recent one by the NCSL had come up with a dollar amount that was based on solid data and could guarantee student success.

In May 2005, possibly in response to a written request from Hogan, Governor Janet Napolitano vetoed House Bill 2718, legislation that included revisions to assessments, additional sources of funding, and other specifics to comply with the *Flores* consent order. One of the several grounds for the veto was the claim that the bill illegally required replacing the funding of state obligations with federal money, a concept known as *supplanting*.[11]

In July 2005, Hogan renewed his contempt motion in federal district court. The Arizona Attorney General's Office and José Cárdenas of the Phoenix firm Lewis & Roca represented the state defendants: the State of Arizona, the Arizona State Board of Education, and State Superintendent of Public Instruction Tom Horne. Cárdenas prepared a response that asked the district court judge to provide the defendants with guidance as to whether the funding scheme amounted to "supplanting."

Horne told Cárdenas that he should ask the court to hold Hogan responsible for the demise of the bill because Hogan had urged Napolitano, in writing, to veto it. In Horne's opinion, because of Hogan's interference, Hogan had no justification to complain about a lack of legislation regarding *Flores*. Horne based his position on the unclean hands doctrine.[12] This doctrine allows the defense to allege that the plaintiff should be disqualified from receiving relief because of an unethical and/or inappropriate action. Neither the attorneys representing the attorney general's office nor Cárdenas agreed with Horne on this issue.

Horne contacted attorney Eric Bistrow, his former law partner who was now with the Phoenix firm Burch & Cracchiolo, to seek his assistance. Bistrow researched the unclean hands doctrine and then consulted with several lawyers in his firm to make sure that this defense would not cause unforeseen ethical issues. They agreed unanimously that it would not.[13]

Bistrow met with Horne and the lawyers for the state in Horne's office. Ultimately, the lawyers agreed to appoint Bistrow to represent Horne in the proceedings, but not beyond raising the unclean hands defense.

DISTRICT COURT PROCEEDINGS

On October 31, 2005, Eric Bistrow participated in the oral arguments at district court in Tucson. José Cárdenas put forth most of the case for the state. Tim Hogan represented the Nogales plaintiffs. US District Judge Raner C. Collins, who had taken over the case due to Judge Marquez's retirement, presided.

Intrigued by Bistrow's argument, Collins asked him, "How did Tim Hogan's brief letter cause Governor Napolitano to veto the bill?"

Bistrow replied, "It is difficult to know what goes on in a governor's head. A governor will always say that she acted in the public interest. What we do know is that Mr. Hogan by letter asked her to veto the bill and that, thereafter, she did so. Consequently, at a minimum, Mr. Hogan's actions aided and abetted the veto of that bill!"[14]

Hogan requested that Collins put a freeze on more than $500 million in federal highway construction funding until the state came up with a reasonable compromise. Ronald Messerly, a lawyer representing a national engineering and general contractors' organization, listed the many freeway projects that would cease should the money be held back, and then threatened an appeal.

An *Arizona Republic* reporter noted that "Collins leaned forward in his chair before dismissing Messerly and asked, 'What course in law school prepares you to tell a judge what he can and can't do?'"[15]

After questioning attorneys on both sides and becoming frustrated by the lack of action to resolve the issue, Collins asked Cárdenas, "Who would you lock up?" He then directed a similar question to Hogan: "So, hypothetically speaking, if we were talking about throwing someone in jail, who would be the first three names off your lips?"[16]

Cárdenas answered that no one should be locked up.

Hogan showed himself to be bipartisan in his choices: "Governor Janet Napolitano [Democrat], Senate President Ken Bennett [Republican] and House Speaker Jim Weiers [Republican]." Hogan argued further that more than 80 percent of ELLs had failed the high-stakes Arizona Instrument to Measure Standards because the funding issue had not been resolved. With that in mind, he requested that ELLs be exempted from the AIMS.[17]

In December 2005, Collins rejected the defendants' arguments. He ordered the Arizona legislature and Governor Janet Napolitano to develop a funding plan for educating ELLs or be fined up to $2 million per day, beginning in March 2006. In addition, he excluded ELLs from having to pass the AIMS as a graduation requirement.

SUPERINTENDENT HORNE'S APPEAL TO CIRCUIT COURT

Horne arranged for Bistrow to handle an appeal to this ruling on Horne's behalf. Bistrow would be representing only the superintendent because the state and the Arizona State Board of Education had decided not to appeal. Horne and Bistrow were on their own in opposing Collins's decision.

According to Bistrow, "During all appellate processes, Tim Hogan continually asked that the appeal be dismissed because the superintendent was not a 'harmed' or 'aggrieved' party, claiming the state, not the superintendent, would ultimately have to pay any fines." Each time Bistrow countered Hogan's complaint, "The superintendent was a party, and, as such, had been found to be in contempt. Therefore, he was 'aggrieved'!"[18]

In January 2006, Bistrow filed a Notice of Appeal to the Ninth Circuit Court in San Francisco. He asked Collins to stay his contempt order pending the outcome of the appeal. In March, the judge refused. Instead, soon after, the Ninth Circuit granted him the stay. By this time, the state had paid more than $20 million in fines into a special account.

OPPOSITION TO THE ELL EXEMPTION IN NOGALES

In late January, Nogales high school English teacher Kathy Scott expressed disagreement with Collins's exemption of ELLs from the AIMS in a column for the *Nogales International*, the town's daily newspaper. According to Scott, Collins's ruling was "an insult to the thousands of ELL students who have indeed shined academically" and was "unfair to non-ELL students who must sit on the sidelines graduation night because they did not reach mastery."[19]

Scott stated further that it was a "fallacy that increased funding alone would account for a higher number of ELL students passing the AIMS." She elaborated that the Nogales students had been offered extra AIMS classes, after-school tutoring, and the use of study guides to help them—all made possible through supplemental funding provided by federal grants. She also believed that treating the fifty-seven ELLs differently from their peers by not holding them accountable "for their own lack of achievement" sent the message that an ELL label was a "ticket to a diploma"—that is, an incentive for ELLs to purposely fail future English proficiency tests.[20]

IMPRESSIVE ACADEMIC IMPROVEMENT

Horne asked assistant superintendent Margaret Garcia Dugan to create a study that would identify all schools with at least one hundred ELLs enrolled. The purpose of this study was to compare the ELLs' scores in English and math on the state achievement test in 2003 with the scores on the test in 2005. After completing the study, Dugan was able to rank approximately seven hundred schools. To their amazement, the study found the ELLs in five of the Nogales schools had scored among the top ten in the state. Bistrow remarked, "How could this be? I thought the ELL programs in Nogales were completely dysfunctional. We need to find out what is going on in Nogales."[21]

At Bistrow's request, Dugan put together a group of experts from the ADE to visit Nogales schools. For three days, they thoroughly investigated the ELL programs at ten Nogales schools. Bistrow recalled that the specifics of the experts' report astounded them:

> Every single deleterious condition described by the United States district court judge in the February 2000 order had been cured. Classrooms were now small. Plentiful instructional materials existed. Teachers were highly competent to instruct English language learners. At least two hours were set aside for such instruction. Computerized programs had been developed to track advances toward English fluency for each ELL student. The bilingual program that had been an abject failure was replaced by a structured English immersion program that required students to be taught in English. The results were remarkable. Objective testing showed that ELL students, who had become proficient in English, outscored native speaking students on Arizona's English and math achievement tests.[22]

A great deal of change had taken place since the original *Flores* complaint. The state had increased general and designated education funding for ELLs substantially. The Nogales voters had enacted overrides that provided additional money for the schools. Most important, in August 2000 the Nogales Unified School District had hired Kelt Cooper to be its new superintendent as part of the community's decision to convert from bilingual to structured English immersion education.

Besides the accomplishments that Bistrow cited from the report, Cooper had ended social promotion, which had become chronic; implemented summer remediation programs; provided accelerated classes for advanced students; raised teachers' salaries by eliminating teacher aides; decreased class size from forty to twenty-two students per class in the early grades; and increased math instruction from one and a half hours per week to one hour every day.

While visiting the Nogales schools in mid-April 2006, I observed many positive factors that had likely contributed to the Nogales district's academic gains:

- The teachers had organized the instruction to such a degree that teachers were able to track the progress of each student. When a student was faltering, steps were taken immediately to bring that student up to par.
- The collaboration between and camaraderie among the teachers led to a sharing of desired outcomes and a variety of methods for reaching them. Whereas the teachers at a particular grade level were teaching the same material, the activities varied considerably based on the individual teacher's personality and the makeup of each class.
- The English language development classes were intense and effectively covered vocabulary as well as elements of morphology.
- Teachers looked upon the students as their children, so their expectations were high. In this small community, everyone was connected through friendships or family ties. As a result, the disregarding of students as "other people's children," often prevalent in inner-city schools, was absent.
- English prevailed in the schools, whereas Spanish was spoken throughout the town. Outside of school, the children spoke both Spanish and English to each other, exhibiting an excellent grasp of both languages. Although bilingual education had disappeared, the students were offered Spanish as an elective from seventh grade through high school.

ENACTMENT OF HOUSE BILL 2064

The legislature passed two more bills regarding ELL education, Senate Bill 1198 and House Bill 2002, between January and March 2006. As she had with HB 2718 in May 2005, Napolitano vetoed both bills, mostly because they established new individual and corporate income tax credits for ELLs to attend private schools. Finally, the legislature passed House Bill 2064, which, unlike the three previous bills, excluded the tax credits for ELLs. It ordered the creation of a nine-member ELL Task Force, to be provided with a staff in the ADE. In addition, it increased funding to $423 per ELL, which was based on a "group B weight" formula and ended for the individual ELL after two years. It remained contingent on the district court's acceptance that the bill fulfilled the consent order.

On March 3, the governor announced that she would allow HB 2064 to become law without her signature but that she would send a letter to Collins expressing her objections to it. She disagreed with ending the per-student state funding after two years because she believed that many ELLs needed more time to learn English. Also, she feared the bill's requirement for schools to use federal funds for ELL programs would prove illegal, and she considered the per-student funding amount to be inadequate.

In an *Arizona Republic* column on March 5, 2006, Napolitano wrote, "Despite my efforts to negotiate a solid English-learner bill—one that not only satisfies the court, but actually works—the Legislature has sent to me a measure that does not satisfy our needs. And although it was tempting to veto this bill for the fourth time, I decided that the Legislature would do no more without judicial intervention."[23]

In the meantime, attorney Eric Bistrow requested a formal evidentiary hearing to present his findings. He included the investigative report from the ELL experts who had visited the Nogales schools and an affidavit from Nogales superintendent Kelt Cooper that described the many improvements Cooper had made since 2000. In addition, he moved the court to vacate the 2000 order on the basis of changed conditions. His request was denied.

On March 13, 2006, Collins ordered that the more than $20 million in daily fines be distributed among school districts. He also ordered the continuation of the ELL exemption from the AIMS graduation requirement. Both of these were in accordance with his 2005 decision. Furthermore, on April 27, 2006, Collins ruled that HB 2064 did not comply with the consent order. As a result Tom Horne—joined by Jim Weiers, speaker of the Arizona House of Representatives, and Ken Bennett, president of the Arizona Senate, as intervenors—filed several appeals to these orders.

THE NINTH CIRCUIT COURT OF APPEALS RESPONDS

In May the US Court of Appeals for the Ninth Circuit set forth a briefing schedule in response to all the appeals. With oral arguments set for late July, Bistrow later remarked that for two months he did nothing "but review and write briefs on issues ranging from constitutional issues to standards requiring courts to grant relief from prior judgments."[24]

Bistrow and David Cantelme, a noted Phoenix lawyer representing the Arizona legislature, presented oral arguments to the circuit court on July 24, 2006. Bistrow felt it went well: "The size of the fine—some $720 million per year—surely must have loomed large with the panel of three judges. The essence of my argument was that the trial court had issued these monstrous fines without even knowing whether problems still existed in Nogales and then denied us a hearing to show that they had all been cured."[25]

The appeals court handed down a decision on August 24, 2006, to remand the case back to the district court in Tucson for an evidentiary hearing, because "the landscape of educational funding has changed significantly" since the 2000 court order.[26] At the same time, the decision threw out the fines Collins had imposed on Arizona and annulled Collins's exemption of the ELLs from the AIMS.

THE EVIDENTIARY HEARING

The subsequent mandatory evidentiary hearing occurred in January 2007 in Tucson. In his memoirs, Bistrow described how he spent a massive amount of time in preparation for the hearing. He put together an entire affirmative case supporting changed conditions, not only in Nogales but in all of Arizona. He named new funding sources that were now available for education generally and specifically for ELL students. He detailed why structured English immersion strategies were superior to those of bilingual education. He demonstrated that each of the deleterious conditions of the 2000 order had been cured.

Bistrow brought forth Irene Moreno, the deputy associate superintendent of the Office of English Language Acquisition Services (OELAS) at the ADE, who had herself entered school as an English learner. She testified that she had worked with ELLs for twenty-seven years in three different Arizona school districts as both a teacher and an administrator.

Moreno considered SEI preferable to bilingual education because of its emphasis on learning English: "You don't teach a student to become a proficient basketball player and not use the basketball. The same way with a pianist. So in order to make them [the students] proficient in the language you use English."[27]

Moreno considered bilingual education to have resulted in a lost opportunity for ELLs and admitted that many teachers did not want to change their ways: "I get them [ELLs] in seventh and eighth grade and they're still in a bilingual program. It's just kind of hard to stomach. There needs to be a shift, and I think that is difficult for people."[28]

When Bistrow asked Moreno about the Proposition 203 clause "temporary transition period, not normally intended to exceed one year," she responded, "If you're doing what you need to do with students, if you're actually teaching, if you're taking those strategies . . . these students learn like other students, they should be able to be out of the program within a year's time. Now, like native English speakers, there may be an issue . . . but everyone should be able to make that transition out within a year's time."[29] [*Note:* Her remarks, based on her years of experience, agreed with Professor Christine Rossell's conclusion based on years of research; see chap. 9, pp. 113–14.]

Moreno elaborated about how her department had brought together groups of teachers and experts to create a state program so ELLs would learn

English and then be able to transfer successfully into mainstream classes. She detailed the following connecting elements of the program:

* Consistent proficiency standards aligned and linked to the state's mainstream language arts standards;
* The Stanford English Language Proficiency (SELP) assessment by Harcourt, which evolved into the Arizona English Language Learner Assessment (AZELLA) that aligned with the proficiency standards;
* The ELL models, developed by Moreno and two other staff members, and aligned with the proficiency standards (The ELL task force would choose and vote on the permanent ELL models in September 2007.];
* An advisory council to revisit the elements of the models;
* The SEI endorsements required of all teachers and administrators;
* Monthly meetings to answer questions and guide the practitioners of ELLs;
* Professional development seminars; and
* The monitoring of ELL programs in schools throughout the state.

At the end of the session, Moreno affirmed the upcoming development and implementation of mandatory ELL models in all school districts and charter schools throughout Arizona as a requirement of HB 2064.[30]

Bistrow then called to the stand Dr. Rosalie Pedalino Porter as expert witness for the defense in the field of English language acquisition. In response to Bistrow's questions, Porter shared her experiences as a teacher, administrator, scholar, and author. She had observed ELLs in "many hundreds, probably over a thousand classrooms."[31] She had sought the best ways of educating these children by researching how other large immigrant-receiving countries such as Germany, Canada, Sweden and Israel resolved their language acquisition challenges.

When asked about bilingual education, Porter responded, "It was meant for all subjects to be taught in the native language in the first few years, with ESL [English as a second language] classes, let's say 30 to 45 minutes every day . . . and that within three years the native language would be reduced, the English teaching would be increased, and we would have a beautiful child ready to do classroom work in English with other kids." She summarized structured English immersion instruction: "It's a very carefully designed program to give intensive English lessons, appropriate to the age of the child . . . to teach the English language so effectively that a child will be able to learn subject matter in English within a short time, a year or two, perhaps three."[32]

When Bistrow asked Porter if an increase in funding provided success for ELLs, she answered that when children need extra help, extra money has to be spent, but the way it is spent is much more important than the amount, because that is where judgment and leadership come in.[33] Later in her testimony, she cited Professor Eric Hanushek of Stanford University, an econo-mist and perhaps the best-known authority on school funding in the country, who concluded in several of his research studies that simply putting in more money does not necessarily equal success.[34]

Porter explained that she had been lead investigator for READ's part of the 2001 ADE cost study, and in that capacity had traveled with a colleague to Nogales to investigate the Nogales Unified School District. She went into detail regarding their interviews with the superintendent, school principals, and teachers during the week spent there. She described the classrooms and teaching materials. She talked about the large amount of data they had col-lected and analyzed. She said that they found no indication that the schools were not being served because of lack of funding.[35]

She expressed her overall impression of the schools: "I have a very high opinion of the Nogales Unified School District for the job it is doing for its ELL students . . . the high level of performance on AIMS, SAT-9 tests, the progress from year to year where improvement is shown, the high level of performance and high percentage of students tested is better than what I have seen in many places in California, Massachusetts and other places. This is just a fine performance."[36]

Attorney Tim Hogan asked Porter in his cross-examination whether there should be a goal for how long it should take ELLs to acquire and become proficient in English. She warned that ELLs have been kept too long in a program, to their detriment:

> If you make the law that these children are to have one to two years [in an ELL program] . . . and you have special funding, a lot of teachers will stretch it to three or four. If you make the law that they're to have three years, they'll stretch it to five. I have experience with this in the state of California where students were kept in bilingual programs not the three years recommended, but five or six beyond the point where they needed English language learning. . . .
> If they're having problems, maybe their reading is not up to grade level, they need special help with reading, but they don't continue to need English lan-guage help.[37]

Hogan did not counter Bistrow's evidence regarding the success of ELLs in the Nogales schools. However, he made the point that some ELLs in Nogales, and especially those in the higher grades in other Arizona school districts, required four to five years to be reclassified as English proficient. Hogan went on to insist that the original judgment declared that the funding system was inadequate and that until that deficiency was corrected, the judg-ment could not be deemed satisfied. Bistrow disagreed, insisting that federal law required results—effective ELL programs—not a specific stream of income.[38]

Collins ruled again in March 2007 that 2064 did not satisfy the court order of January 2000. It violated federal law by supplanting federal dollars and requiring a two-year maximum per-student funding limitation.[39] Collins gave the state until the end of 2007 to comply with the original *Flores* consent order of 2000.

Arizona Republic columnist Robert Robb lambasted Collins's decision, explaining that the lawsuit had always been "a fool's errand" because there was "no magical figure" that "if spent, would make the achievement gap between English learners and native speakers disappear." Robb explained further that the "underpinnings" of the *Flores* lawsuit had always been "the poor performance of Nogales students on standardized tests."[40]

Robb criticized Collins for overlooking the fact that the Nogales ELLs "were becoming proficient and scoring above state averages on the AIMS." That Collins had discounted the impressive academic improvement of ELLs as well as the additional federal, state, and local resources that had poured into Nogales schools constituted, according to Robb, "the most amazing adventure yet in this legal Neverland."[41]

Rather than comply with Collins's deadline, the attorneys for the state appealed his order again to the Ninth Circuit Court of Appeals, which, in turn, ruled against the state and in favor of the respondents on February 22. As a result, in September 2008, Bistrow, on behalf of Horne and Arizona Speaker of the House Jim Weiers, petitioned the US Supreme Court to review the circuit court's decision—a long shot because the Supreme Court receives about seven thousand petitions every year and accepts approximately 1 percent of them.

US SUPREME COURT HEARS THE *FLORES* CASE

On January 9, 2009, the Supreme Court agreed to hear separate appeals filed by Horne, through his attorney Eric Bistrow, and by the Arizona State Legislature, through its attorney Ken Starr. According to the appeal written partly by Starr, a former US solicitor general and independent counsel, "Arizona needs this court's help to return control over the funding of Arizona's school programs to where it rightly belongs—out of the hands of a single federal district court judge and back into the hands of Arizona's democratically accountable officials."[42]

Bistrow and Starr planned to divide the opening argument, and Starr would then handle the rebuttal. They had to seek a formal order that allowed them to have dual arguments. About a week before oral argument, the Supreme Court denied the dual argument for Bistrow and Starr but granted it for the respondents. Bistrow was disappointed; he could not understand the rationale for doing this.[43]

Horne and Bistrow both decided that it would serve the state's interests to have Starr argue the case. Bistrow spent a day providing Starr with extensive background and briefing on the case. In addition, Bistrow served on a moot court, asking Starr questions and critiquing his answers. [44]

ORAL ARGUMENTS BEFORE THE COURT

The US Supreme Court heard *Thomas C. Horne, Superintendent, Arizona Public Instruction, Petitioner, v. Miriam Flores, et al.* (No. 08-289) and *Speaker of the Arizona House of Representatives, Petitioner, v. Miriam Flores, et al.* (No. 08-294) on April 20, 2009. The quotations from those proceedings that appear below have been taken from the "Official—Subject to Final Review" account. [45]

Starr made the following points on behalf of the petitioners:

- Since the original *Flores* lawsuit, a "sea change" had occurred in education policy in Arizona. The old system in Nogales was done away with throughout the state due to the voters' approval of Proposition 203 in 2000 that replaced bilingual education with "intense immersion" and the requirements of the federal No Child Left Behind Act that passed in 2001.
- The fact that the elected Arizona officials (Superintendent Lisa Graham Keegan, Attorney General Janet Napolitano, and Governor Jane Hull) at the time did not appeal the district court ruling of 2000 "should be in fact a cause for concern."
- The new leadership of Nogales schools led by Superintendent Kelt Cooper had brought in additional "changed circumstances." According to the Ninth Circuit, Nogales was doing "substantially better" and the state had developed "a significantly improved infrastructure." The key would be to measure that progress.
- The increase in funding, as established in House Bill 2064, was substantial in that it had paid for "an effective program" in Nogales.
- Contrary to the accusation, there had been "good faith efforts toward compliance" with the *Flores* consent order. [46]

Justice David Souter laid out what he viewed as the problems with HB 2064:

- HB 2064 had limited the funding to two years, when evidence showed two years to be not enough to "get a kid up to par."
- Federal funds were being used to supplant rather than merely supplement the costs for educating ELLs. [47]

Justice Anthony Kennedy asked whether any remedy based on funding was inappropriate due to the methodology of No Child Left Behind. Starr explained, "A funding remedy is in fact inappropriate presumptively state-wide." He continued, "That is our key submission, because of the variation in costs, district by district." After further discussion, Starr added that "the oddity about this case" was that the district court had not determined whether there was an ineffective program in place for the entire state when it ruled the remedy must be statewide.[48]

Starr explained further that the district court had failed to note the change from bilingual to immersion education, "which has an entirely different methodology." He pointed out that the district court acknowledged "a signifi-cantly improved infrastructure for ELL programming," but still held that the state had "not complied with the original judgment." He gave an example: "Superintendent Cooper comes in and says, 'I don't want to spend money on teachers' aides; they are standing in the way.' Yet the respondents say, 'We need money for teachers' aides. That's part of No Child Left Behind.'"[49]

Starr elaborated that "the entire State funding mechanism had been inter-fered with by the order" and that the NCSL had given up on its cost study because they could not do it statewide. Starr argued that only Nogales should be considered in the lawsuit.[50]

Justice Antonin Scalia questioned the attorney general's intent "to fund the whole State . . . to fix Nogales." He pointed out that there exist "vast" differences among the Arizona school districts.[51]

Sri Srinivasan, a native of India and noted lecturer at Harvard Law School, argued the case on behalf of the respondents. He admitted that the achievement of ELLs in Nogales had improved in most grades, but noted that they had not at the high school level. He added that it was premature to make assessments of the changes because new standards were still evolving. He explained that "in order to justify complete dissolution [of the *Flores* consent order] in a case like this, the Petitioners would have to show, not only that conditions have improved, but they have improved in a way that is durable and sustainable over time."[52]

Scalia asked, "What degree of improvement do you think is necessary?" and "Do you really think that you haven't complied with adequate funding of ELL programs until you raise all of the ELL students up to the level of native English speakers?"[53]

Srinivasan responded negatively and then elaborated that the two Nogales high schools had ranked at the very bottom of the survey for ELL students. He stated further that the so-called new plan occurred because of HB 2064. He urged that the court "fortify the district court's conclusion that complete dissolution [of HB 2064] was warranted" for these reasons:

- No matter the progress to date, it did not suffice because the net effect of HB 2064 was to decrease the resources by half.
- It was premature to make an assessment until enough time had passed to determine what had happened on the ground as a consequence [of HB 2064].[54]

Chief Justice John Roberts inquired, "[D]oes that stay true without regard to what is happening economically to the State? In other words, the district court can say, 'You've got to spend this much money on this program, and I don't care what it means for jails, roads, anything else, when there are profound changes in economic circumstances of the sort that everybody's experiencing lately.'"[55]

After Srinivasan answered that the state would have to make the argument that funding constraints were in existence that did not allow for an optimal program, Scalia exclaimed:

> I find it bizarre that we are sitting here talking about what the whole State has to do on the basis of one district which is concededly the district that has the most non-native English speakers and has been a problem district all along. And we are saying whatever this district court says for this school district applies statewide. . . . And the mere fact that the State Attorney General acquiesced in that kind of a system at the outset, does that force us to still accept at this time that whatever is necessary for Nogales is also necessary for the entire State?[56]

Scalia, Kennedy, and Roberts continued to express dismay that the remedies to the problems found in Nogales schools had been applied to the entire state. They considered this to have happened because of former attorney general Janet Napolitano's questionable interpretation of the Arizona constitution's "equality clause."[57]

THE AMICUS CURIAE BRIEF

As an amicus curiae representing the United States and President Barack Obama, the solicitor general's assistant Nicole A. Saharsky presented arguments on behalf of the respondents and in support of the Ninth Circuit Court ruling. She focused on the district court's eight-day evidentiary hearing that she said made factual findings that the troubles in Nogales had continued.

Saharsky outlined three specific problems with HB 2064: The two-year cutoff of funding; the use of federal funds "to supplant, not supplement"; and the state's allotment of $450 per ELL, which she described as insufficient. In addition, she noted that the respondents had not come up with a cost study during the nine years since the original *Flores* judgment regarding how much a good program would cost.[58]

THE COURT'S 5–4 DECISION FAVORS THE STATE

Justice Samuel Alito wrote for the majority. He was joined by Chief Justice John Roberts, and justices Antonin Scalia, Anthony Kennedy, and Clarence Thomas. He criticized the lower court for not engaging in a particular "Rule" adequately and for keeping to a standard that was "too strict":

> Rather than applying a flexible standard that seeks to return control to state and local officials as soon as a violation of federal law has been remedied, the Court of Appeals used a heightened standard that paid insufficient attention to federalism concerns. And rather than inquiring broadly into whether changed conditions in Nogales provided evidence of an ELL program that complied with the EEOA, the Court of Appeals concerned itself only with determining whether increased ELL funding complied with the original declaratory judgment order. The court erred on both counts.[59]

Alito named the specific "changed circumstances":

- Arizona voters passed Proposition 203, which mandated statewide implementation of a SEI approach, in November 2000.
- In HB 2064, the state legislature had implemented SEI as follows: (1) it had created the Arizona ELL Task Force that developed and adopted research based models of SEI programs; (2) it had required that all school districts and charter schools select one of the adopted SEI models; (3) it had created an Office of English Language Acquisition Services to aid school districts in its implementation of the models; and (4) it had required the State Board of Education to institute a uniform and mandatory training program for all SEI instructors.
- Congress had enacted No Child Left Behind, which requires states to make sure that ELL students "attain English proficiency, develop high levels of academic attainment in English, and meet the same challenging State academic standards as all children are expected to meet," in 2001.
- States must set annual objective achievement goals for the students to progress toward proficiency, achieve proficiency, and make "adequate yearly progress" with respect to academic achievement. Also, it holds local schools and agencies accountable for meeting these objectives.
- Reforms were led by Kelt Cooper, the Nogales superintendent from 2000 to 2005, who "adopted policies that ameliorated or eliminated many of the most glaring inadequacies discussed by the district court."[60]

According to Alito, the lower courts and the dissenters had "misperceived both the nature of the obligation imposed by the EEOA and the breadth of the inquiry." He ordered that the cases be remanded back to the district court for a proper examination of "four important factual and legal changes that may warrant the granting of relief from the judgment [Flores Consent Order, 2000]: The State's adoption of a new ELL instructional methodology, Congress's enactment of NCLB, structural and management reforms in Nogales, and increased over-all education funding."[61]

Alito stated that there were no factual findings that any school district other than Nogales failed to provide equal educational opportunities to ELL students. In other words, the respondents had not explained how a statewide injunction could be justified because of the EEOA. Alito ruled, "Unless the District Court concludes that Arizona is violating the EEOA statewide, it should vacate the injunction insofar as it extends beyond Nogales."[62]

THE COURT'S DISSENTING OPINION

Justice Stephen Breyer dissented and was joined by justices John Paul Stevens, David Souter, and Ruth Bader Ginsburg regarding the State's claim of "changed circumstances":

> The lower courts did "fairly consider" every change in circumstances that the parties called to their attention. The record more than adequately supports this conclusion. In a word, I fear that the Court misapplies an inappropriate procedural framework, reaching a result that neither the record nor the law adequately supports. In doing so, it risks denying schoolchildren the English-learning instruction necessary "to overcome language barriers that impede" their "equal participation."[63]

Breyer objected also to the court's order that the district court "vacate the injunction insofar as it extends beyond Nogales":

> Nothing in the law, as far as I know, makes the relief somehow clearly erroneous. Indeed, as the majority recognizes, the reason that the injunction runs statewide is that the State of Arizona, the defendant in the litigation, *asked the Court to enter that relief.* The State pointed to a state constitutional provision requiring educational uniformity. . . . There is no indication that anyone disputed whether the injunction should have statewide scope. A statewide program harmed Nogales' students . . . and the State wanted statewide relief. What in the law makes this relief erroneous?[64]

RESPONSES TO THE US SUPREME COURT DECISION

Arizona Republic writer Pat Kossan explained that the high court's 5–4 decision had "taken a major step towards ending a 17-year legal battle" by reversing the federal appeals court ruling that Arizona needed to improve its funding of ELL instruction.[65] As a result, Arizona would no longer need to fear that the lower court would impose multimillion-dollar daily fines on the state for noncompliance.

Superintendent Tom Horne's press secretary issued a release on June 25, 2009, that included a quote from Horne: "The U.S. Supreme Court has taken a major step to stop federal district judges from micromanaging the state's education systems. We the people should rule ourselves through our elected representatives and should not be ruled by an aristocracy of lifetime federal judges. By its ruling, the U.S. Supreme Court reaffirmed this important principle."

Attorney Tim Hogan admitted he was disappointed in the decision reversing that of the appeals court, but added that remanding the case back to the lower court would keep the legal battle alive. He stated further, "This will give us an opportunity now to fully test the existing program that's in place for English language learners in Arizona and whether or not that program is working."[66] Hogan was talking about the SEI models of instruction created by the Arizona ELL Task Force to fulfill requirements of HB 2064, Prop 203, the *Flores* consent order, and No Child Left Behind.

FLORES RETURNS TO DISTRICT COURT FOR THE LAST TIME

In the fall of 2010, Hogan took the case back to the US District Court in Tucson to be heard once again before Judge Raner Collins. He reversed his earlier approach, insisting that the state's mandatory SEI instructional models were not acceptable. He said that the practice of grouping ELLs for four hours of English until they had passed a high-stakes test was deeply flawed, especially for those ELLs who failed to test out of the program after the first year. He claimed it constituted "impermissible segregation in violation of the Fourteenth Amendment to the Constitution" and "created permanent academic deficits in other areas such as the arts, social studies, and science."[67]

Hogan brought forth expert academics from universities in Arizona and California to back up his objections to the ELL models. The academics claimed their conclusions were based on specific studies; however, they were unwilling to provide the data to back up their conclusions, even after Collins required them to do so. Consequently, Hogan proceeded to trial without a single one of the so-called experts.[68]

Attorney Eric Bistrow put on the witness stand many teachers and principals as well as the superintendent of the Nogales Unified School District. They praised the SEI program and denied all of Hogan's charges. They testified that ELLs intermingled well with their English-dominant peers, and that they were neither demeaned nor segregated.

THE *FLORES* CASE IS RESOLVED

More than two years later, on March 28, 2013, Collins granted the state relief and determined that the original 2000 order would no longer be enforced. The Ninth Circuit Court of Appeals complied with the ruling in June 2015.

Finally, after twenty-three years, the *Flores* lawsuit had come to a close. The arguments of Superintendent Tom Horne and attorney Eric Bistrow had prevailed.

The wider lessons taught by this lawsuit are of crucial importance for educators of the more than 5 million children entering our schools without sufficient command of the English language to do regular classroom work in English. Both sides of the issue proclaimed the fundamental educational needs of this population of children.

Essential for all ELLs across the country is the fact that the majority and dissenting opinions agreed on two principles: the federal requirement to teach English to ELLs for full participation so that "linguistic diversity can support rather than undermine our democratic institutions," and a documented, academic support for the view that structured English immersion is significantly more effective than bilingual education.

Chapter Six

Implementing Structured English Immersion

Arizona is the only state to attempt to fully implement sheltered or structured English immersion in all of its school districts and charter schools where English language learners are in attendance. The state is following a provision of Arizona Proposition 203 that requires schools to place ELLs together in classrooms divided according to their degree of fluency to learn English through SEI techniques.

In accordance with Prop 203, the policy makers at the Arizona Department of Education concluded that most of the ELLs would be better off in mainstream classrooms than in separate SEI classrooms after about a year, although they would still need extra help in reading and writing. Thus they opted for "proficiency" to be a composite score on the Arizona English Language Learner Assessment that put more weight on the oral/listening than on the reading and writing subtests. At the same time, it became a requirement for state certification that all Arizona mainstream teachers receive SEI training to accommodate the former ELLs as they transferred into their classes.

THE HOUSE BILL 2064 REQUIREMENTS

In 2006, in compliance with the *Flores* consent order and Prop 203, Arizona House Bill 2064 authorized the creation of a nine-member Arizona ELL Task Force established within the ADE and provided with ADE staff support. The task force members would serve four-year terms and were chosen by Arizona state government officials: three members by the superintendent of public instruction, two members by the governor, two members by the House of

Representatives, and two members by the Senate. The task force was responsible for items related to the development, adoption, and continual monitoring of the most cost-effective research-based SEI models that agreed with state and federal laws.[1]

The task force assembled for six years, from September 2006 to May 2012. Throughout that time, three members remained active participants: Alan Maguire (chairman), acclaimed economist and frequent advisor to government officeholders on policy regarding finance; Margaret Garcia Dugan, Arizona deputy superintendent and former Proposition 203 cochair; and, Johanna Haver, author of this book. The other members on the task force held positions as administrators or teachers in various parts of the state. Some worked in the Arizona legislature or the Arizona Department of Education. One member, Eugene Garcia, was former dean of the Arizona State University College of Education.

The Office of English Language Acquisition Services was created to carry out the policy decisions of the task force and to help school districts and charter schools implement the new models. The responsibilities of OELAS included developing and publishing of guidelines, consulting with county officials to develop regional programs, providing technical assistance and teacher training, and continually monitoring ELL programs. Moreover, OELAS officials were expected to keep the task force and the ADE abreast of their findings and progress.[2]

In accordance with HB 2064, the SEI models had to include four hours daily of English language development (ELD) for the first year in which a pupil was classified as an ELL. School district and charter schools would be allowed to implement alternative models if approved by the task force.

PRESENTATIONS FROM ELL PRACTITIONERS

The members of the task force decided to examine what appeared to be SEI programs currently in operation and requested that the ADE arrange for school districts and charter schools to give presentations about their programs. The members specified that they wanted to see how schools were dealing with special situations such as Native-American ELLs, low enrollment of ELLs, and high refugee populations. In addition, they requested that schools from urban, rural, and border districts be represented. They realized that the ELL models had to encompass all possible situations.[3]

During the first five meetings in September and October of 2006, and then frequently throughout 2007, the task force heard descriptions of dozens of programs that included single schools, entire districts, and charter school organizations. The teachers and program directors talked about their instructional models, which consisted of variations of the following: separate instruction in ELD daily for one to three hours, content-area classes exclusively for ELLs in a sheltered setting, and accommodations for ELLs in mainstream classes where ELLs were combined with non-ELLs.

In several elementary schools, ELLs received their reading instruction with non-ELLs in small ability-based groupings through systematic phonics-based programs such as Success for All and Reading First, national programs that had proven especially effective for ELLs. The ELLs were well integrated among the non-ELLs during this ninety-minute-per-day instruction because, like the non-ELLs, their reading abilities ranged from poor to excellent. The fact that ELLs did not necessarily fall into low-ability reading groups was an indication that ELLs are better off being taught reading in mainstream classrooms, rather than in a separate setting.

The schools differed with regard to the average time it took their ELLs to reach proficiency. Usually elementary-age ELLs qualified for mainstreaming after two or three years, whereas this process could take as long as five years for older children, especially for illiterate new immigrant ELLs enrolled in high school. Understandably, high school students took the longest because of the high academic level of the material they were expected to master.

ELLs in a school with mostly non-ELLs advanced more rapidly than those in schools where the majority of the students were ELLs. The smaller the number of ELLs, the greater the opportunity and incentive for them to practice their English.

REACHING CONSENSUS

Some teachers expressed opposition to imposing four-hour SEI models on ELLs because they feared if all newcomers were placed in one classroom, they would socialize only with themselves, even during recess and playtime. They would rely on their native language rather than using their new language, English. Other school practitioners agreed with the plan of segregating the ELLs from the others for at least part of the day because this would make it easier for the teachers to create ELD lessons to meet the specific linguistic needs of ELLs. ELLs would be less inhibited to express themselves among other ELLs than in a setting of mostly non-ELLs, where they may not understand the language surrounding them.[4]

Both HB 2064 and Prop 203 specified a period of one year, with the goal that ELLs become proficient in English and transition to mainstream classes as quickly as possible. The members of the task force appeared to understand that keeping ELLs too long in ELD classes could be as damaging to them as not providing any special instruction in the first place.

SUGGESTIONS FROM THE EXPERTS

In November 2006 the chairman of the task force brought forth leading professors of education to do presentations and answer questions of the members regarding the education of ELLs. The presenters were Dr. Richard Ruiz, professor of language, reading, and culture and head of the Department of Teaching and Teacher Education at the University of Arizona; Dr. Christian Faltis, professor of education in the Division of Curriculum and Instruction at the Mary Lou Fulton College of Education at Arizona State University; and Dr. Norbert Francis, associate professor of bilingual/multicultural education at the College of Education at Northern Arizona University.

The professors offered some specific suggestions, including:

- ELL programs should facilitate opportunities to use the language being learned in different contexts and functions, so that one is not merely learning a language for the sake of learning a language. (Ruiz)
- Two assessments are preferable: one for placement and one for reclassification, specifically the AZELLA for placement and the state-mandated Arizona Instrument to Measure Standards for reclassification. (Faltis)
- Whereas all ELL programs could be effective, the project summary of the Carnegie Corporation research "Double the Work" supports immersion overall as the most effective way to learn a second language, especially while being taught through content. (Francis)
- Math and science, with a language-development emphasis, could also be considered as part of the four-hour instruction. Universities need more classes in teaching content through language development methodologies. (Francis)[5]

RECOMMENDATIONS FROM THREE SEI EXPERTS

On November 30, 2006, the chairman introduced to the task force three SEI experts: Kevin Clark, senior consultant with Clark Consulting and Training; Dr. Rosalie Pedalino Porter, director of the Institute for Research in English Acquisition and Development and former cochair of English for the Children in Massachusetts; and Dr. Ken Noonan, superintendent of California Oceanside Unified School District, which had transitioned successfully from bilingual to immersion education after California Prop 227 passed in 1998.

The three experts answered questions and provided firsthand information about schools where ELLs' achievement levels had improved as a result of SEI instruction. They discussed the importance of parental involvement, community backing, teacher training, after-school/summer programs, and making sure ELLs spend a good portion of the day with non-ELLs. They suggested ways to encourage colleges of education to include SEI practices in their curriculum.

Kevin Clark explained that he had worked with many school districts in implementing SEI programs. He understood it was the mission of the task force to help schools move toward compliance with the law.

Clark named important elements of teaching a language, including phonemic awareness, syntax, verb tenses, and vocabulary building. He showed a chart that illustrated a breakdown of four hours of ELD that consisted of twenty minutes of pronunciation, thirty minutes of sentence structure, fifty minutes of vocabulary, up to ninety minutes of reading, and sixty minutes of writing as an example of how SEI could be set up.

Clark convinced most members at the meeting that he could help them reach their goal of developing educationally sound SEI models that corresponded to HB 2064. From that day forward, Kevin Clark worked closely with the task force for this purpose.[6]

DEVELOPMENT OF SEI MODELS AND TEACHER TRAINING

The members discussed and then adopted in May 2007 an SEI model that consisted of four hours of ELD. They submitted this draft model to the Arizona Legislature for review and then held public hearings. The model included the following:

- The identification, placement, and reclassification of ELLs would be determined solely by the students' scores on the state-mandated AZELLA, which would provide a composite proficiency level score as well as separate subtest scores for listening, speaking, reading, and total writing. The test would be administered at least twice, in the fall and in the spring, to first-year ELLs, and once in the spring to continuing students. It would be permissible to administer the AZELLA to an ELL at a midpoint for the purpose of measuring that specific student's progress; however, no student would be allowed to take the AZELLA more than three times in a school year.
- ELLs would be placed in SEI classrooms according to their proficiency levels.
- The SEI content of four hours daily of ELD would focus on the teaching of the English language, as distinguished from the content of a particular subject such as science or history.
- The scheduling and time allocations of the four-hour ELD instruction would be divided according to proficiency and grade levels.
- The class instruction, textbooks, materials, and assessments would align with specific categories of skills identified in the Arizona K–12 ELL

Proficiency Standards, which would be further refined as needed by the Discrete Skills Inventory (DSI).

- SEI classroom teachers would be required to have the same certification as regular teachers at the elementary, middle school, and high school levels.
- All SEI classroom teachers would receive training on DSI implementation and teaching methods. In fact, the full SEI endorsement would be required of all Arizona teachers and administrators. [7]

This model was accepted by the task force on September 13, 2007, and was approved for funding by the Arizona Legislature on April 14, 2008. Only one correction was made to the original draft model: Charter school SEI teachers would be exempt from the requirement to hold the same certification as teachers in traditional public schools.

To this day, three sets of training are mandated for all SEI classroom teachers; school officials and administrators must receive one set designated "implementation training." [8]

ALTERNATIVES TO THE SEI MODEL

During the 2007–2008 school year, the task force created two alternative SEI models for high school. Pending approval by the task force, a school district could implement either the alternative model of the Glendale Union High School District or that for the Phoenix Union High School District. The Glendale model allows a reduction of ELD hours from four to two or three for intermediate ELLs who have scored "approaches the standard" on the AIMS test and have a grade of C or better in core subjects. The Phoenix model allows basic and intermediate ELLs to receive their ELD reading instruction through content-based texts and then earn high school credits in those content areas.

Individual language learner plans (ILLPs) are required if fewer than twenty ELLs are identified in a band consisting of three consecutive grades. Through these ILLPs, teachers can make sure their ELLs receive the mandated four hours of ELD. The teachers can do this by adjusting their instruction to include strategies helpful to all students, although designed for ELLs. The advantage of ILLPs is that ELLs are integrated with mainstream students.

PILOT PROGRAMS

During the 2007–2008 school year, many districts implemented the models to some degree, although they were not required to. Three school districts volunteered to implement the SEI models in their entirety: Glendale Elementary, Humboldt Unified, and Florence Unified.

According to ADE data, the percentage of students testing proficient on the AZELLA in those schools had more than doubled by the end of that school year when compared to the ELL scores of the previous year.[9] In other words, there was reason to believe that the models could improve ELL achievement throughout Arizona. Thus, beginning with the 2008–2009 school year, all Arizona public schools with ELLs were mandated to implement the Arizona SEI models.

STUDENT PROGRESS

By 2008 the ADE data showed that the ELLs at the beginning levels "pre-emergent" and "emergent" were moving rapidly to the third "basic" level, where they were likewise progressing at a decent pace. However, an unacceptably large percentage of ELLs—as many as 66 percent of all ELLs in Arizona—were becoming stuck at the "intermediate" level, the final stage before "proficiency."[10]

The Office of English Language Acquisition Services requested and received backing to launch the Arizona High Intensity Summer ELD Program in 2009, which focused on bringing intermediate-level students to proficiency. As a result, six school districts with large numbers of ELLs provided instruction exclusively for intermediate-level ELLs in grades 2–8 at their school sites for six hours per day over twenty days.

As a member of the ELL task force, I personally observed classes at two different schools and was impressed to see small children fully engaged in putting together complex sentences and increasing their vocabularies with words that expressed complex concepts. The idea was to move them beyond their comfort level of everyday English communication into the higher-level language needed for academic pursuits.

The program appeared successful and proved that children—specifically ELLs—are capable of learning a great deal more than previously thought if the instruction is both motivational and well organized. Some 44 percent of the ELL participants, or 152 out of 349, reached English proficiency, as measured by the AZELLA results, by the end of the twenty days.[11]

PROGRESS CONTINUES

The outcomes were looking positive. According to ADE data, the ELL reclassification rate had increased from 24 to 34.7 percent in the two years since the model's implementation. In addition, the students identified as fluent English proficient who continued to be administered the AZELLA for two years after scoring "proficient," in accordance with the law, were reported to be passing the AIMS on average at 64 percent in math and 71 percent in reading.[12]

COMPLAINTS ABOUT SEI MODELS

Many ELL instructors, program directors, and school administrators, however, found fault with the highly prescribed models. They protested through letters to the ADE and appearances at task force meetings. Specific complaints included:

- The models are too prescriptive in that they specify the exact number of hours, type of instruction, and teaching methods. Such restriction could not possibly meet the needs of every child.
- Four hours of ELD instruction is excessive in that the ELLs are allowed only two hours of daily non-ELD instruction. It becomes impossible for them to receive sufficient instruction in required courses, especially in grades 3 and up, to progress and graduate from high school within a reasonable amount of time.
- Separating ELLs from non-ELLs is a form of segregation that keeps ELLs from participating in the critical thinking that goes on in mainstream classes and denies them the important interaction with proficient English speakers.[13]

THE MOST CONTENTIOUS ISSUE: THE FOUR-HOUR MANDATE

The task force members could not come to an agreement on whether or not the four-hour separation from mainstream instruction should continue indefinitely. Some members feared that interfering with the models in any way would hinder their effectiveness. Other members, mostly those with teaching experience, felt strongly that ELLs should experience more time in mainstream classes, where they would mix with non-ELLs.

In the spring of 2013, the task force disbanded and the Arizona Board of Eductation assumed responsibility for the implementation of the SEI models. The following year, the board set up two committees—one at the elementary level and the other at the secondary level—that created "refinements." As a result, SEI blocks became less rigid, combining skills such as reading with conversation and vocabulary building. Most important, hours could be reduced from four to three in grades K–8 and from four to two in high school for ELLs not quite at the English proficiency level.

IMPROVEMENT CONTINUES

The number of LEP students declined from 112,522 in 1999 to 83,500 in 2017, a reduction from 15 to 7 percent of the total student population. Approximately 73 percent of ELLs are Spanish speakers, and, in general, 45 to 47 percent of the total students in Arizona public schools are Hispanic, with that percentage increasing every year. Speakers of Arabic comprise the second largest language group, varying from 2 to 3 percent of the entire ELL population since the 2012–2013 school year.[14]

Like California, Arizona has made impressive improvements in preparing ELLs for the mainstream and moving them there at a reasonable rate. Whereas only 4 percent of ELLs were reclassified as English proficient in Arizona in 1999, on average 29 percent of ELLs made the cut as English proficient annually between the 2007–2008 to 2014–2015 school years. This is especially significant because Arizona was harder hit than most states by the recession that began in late 2008. Low teacher pay and excessive regulations led to thousands of teachers either moving to other states or exiting the profession altogether. In the fall of school year 2017–2018, approximately eighteen hundred classes were still without instructors.

On average, between the 2007–2008 and 2014–2015 school years, Arizona's monitored former limited English proficient students who had been reclassified and mainstreamed for one to two years scored proficient at a lower rate than all students in Arizona in both reading (65 versus 70 percent) and in math (55 versus 60 percent).[15] A difference of 5 percentage points is not significant because a large proportion of ELLs attend low-performing schools in which non-ELL students also score considerably lower than those in schools where achievement is average or above average. It would be more appropriate to compare the ELLs to non-ELLs at the same school or district, but that data was not available.

In 2016, Arizona seniors graduated from high school at a rate of 79.5 percent, whereas only 32 percent of students classified as ELLs received diplomas that year. However, it is important to note that the percentage of total ELLs who were still classified as such in high school had dwindled to 6 percent of the total in ninth grade, 3 percent in tenth grade, 2 percent in eleventh grade, and 1 percent in twelfth grade. This means that only 568 ELL seniors in high school failed to graduate—a very small number when compared to the entire 1.1 million student population in Arizona.[16]

Information was not available regarding whether high school ELLs dropped out or became reclassified while in high school, nor how many ELLs were new arrivals or had been in the program for more than five years. However, it seems highly likely that the refinements could result in a larger percentage of ELLs sticking with their high school programs and earning diplomas.

PROMOTING BILINGUALISM IN NOGALES HIGH SCHOOL

At the US Supreme Court hearing of the *Flores* lawsuit in 2009, the justices discussed the astounding improvement of the children's academic progress in Nogales elementary schools, most likely due to the school district's switch from bilingual education to structured English immersion. The justices also expressed concern that the high school students were not doing as well.

Since then, improvements have been made at Nogales High School (NHS), the main high school that serves 1,755 students in grades 9–12. Ninety-eight percent of NHS students are identified as low-income and Hispanic, with more than 90 percent identified at one time as ELLs. They have been graduating at a rate of 96 percent annually—19 to 20 percentage points above the state average. The Great Schools website gives Nogales High School 9 points out of 10 for its curricula, noting that the school is "far above the state average in key areas of college and career readiness."[17] According to *US News & World Report*, 32 percent of Nogales students completed Advanced Placement (AP) courses and 47 percent of them passed them in 2018.[18]

As children growing up mostly in Spanish-speaking homes and neighborhoods while at the same time attending schools in which instruction is exclusively in English, they have experienced the ideal situation for becoming fully bilingual, in accordance with the research completed by Professor Joseph Guzman (see introduction, p. xxvi).

To further the development of their bilingualism, Nogales students have the opportunity in sixth grade to study Spanish as an elective and to continue with that language to various degrees throughout middle school and high school. This prepares them for participation in the highly prestigious, academically rigorous International Baccalaureate (IB) program, as lifelong bilingualism is a huge advantage in obtaining an IB diploma.

Nogales school authorities deserve praise for providing their students this opportunity. In the spring of 2017, seven NHS students succeeded in earning IB diplomas. This program, paired with AP credits, offers students entry into the world's most highly rated universities and/or college-level credits for as many as two years of study.

MARICOPA COUNTY COMMUNITY COLLEGES OFFER OPPORTUNITIES

According to the US Census Bureau, the population of Arizona was 6.9 million in 2016. Maricopa County, the largest in the state, had a population of 4.2 million people; 31 percent identified as Hispanic.

The Maricopa County Community College District (MCCCD), one of the largest and most reputable community college systems in the United States, serves mostly the citizens of the greater Phoenix area. MCCCD is comprised of ten regionally accredited colleges with more than thirty campuses located throughout the county that serve the needs of students quite effectively. In fact, Michael Crowe, the president of Arizona State University, has often remarked that students who transfer from MCCCD in their junior year do better academically than students at the junior level who entered ASU as freshmen. This is likely because classes in the Maricopa community colleges are much smaller than those in universities, so students receive individual attention from highly competent instructors who love to teach.

Fortunately, MCCCD has become an excellent solution for an increasing proportion of the former ELLs, even those who have not earned a high school diploma but are above the age of eighteen. According to MCCCD data, the enrollment of Hispanic students in Maricopa community colleges increased from 26 percent (33,335 students) of the total enrollment in 2014 to 33 percent (39,707 students) in 2017. Approximately 2,540 of those students were "Dreamers"—undocumented immigrants who were brought into the United States as children and protected by the Deferred Action for Childhood Arrivals (DACA) program. From 2015 to 2017, approximately 45 percent of Hispanic students identified themselves as having grown up in Spanish-speaking homes, so they were likely ELLs while attending K–12 Arizona schools.

Year after year, these students have shown up at the Maricopa community colleges better prepared for college work than those who enrolled the year before, as demonstrated by their success regarding retention, college-level course completion, and developmental (remedial) course work.

The retention rate for Hispanic students improved from 56 percent in 2011 to 60 percent in 2015, compared to that of white students, which increased from 60 percent in 2011 to 61 percent in 2015. Hispanic students' rate at college-level course success, that is, the percent of students who passed college-level classes for which they received credits rather than "developmental" classes for which the students received no credit, rose from 70 percent in 2011 to 76 percent in 2015, whereas white students' rate improved from 73 percent in 2011 to 79 percent in 2015.

In fall of 2011, 65 percent of Hispanics and 68 percent of whites succeeded in developmental English coursework; both groups succeeded at 73 percent in 2016. Both Hispanics and whites met the developmental reading success mark at 74 percent in 2011 and at 81 percent in 2016. Whites did better in developmental math (62 percent in 2011 and 67 percent in 2016) compared to Hispanics (57 percent in 2011 and 61 percent in 2016). Thus Hispanic students are measuring up to white students in developmental English and reading, but their success rate in developmental math appears to be 5 or 6 percentage points behind that of white students.

What matters most is that Hispanic students—especially those identified as former ELLs, who used to have little chance of academic success even in high school due to their lack of English skills—are doing remarkably better in that they have become competitive with white students.

Chapter Seven

Resistance to Change in New York City

In December 2000, about one month after Arizona passed Proposition 203, Ron Unz ate lunch with *Sacramento Bee* reporter Daniel Weintraub at a Chinese restaurant in Palo Alto, California. Exuberant over his recent Arizona win, Unz became so animated in talking about his crusade to dismantle bilingual education that people at a nearby table moved to the other side of the room. A couple sitting behind the two men later stopped by the men's table to admit that they had been listening in to their conversation and had found it quite interesting.

Unz was explaining to the reporter that he had hoped for a 70 percent win in Arizona before the opponents of Prop 203 convinced Native Americans that the initiative would end their native language programs. He said this wasn't true, but voters nevertheless believed it and changed their minds about supporting Prop 203 at the last minute.

Unz elaborated further, "I really want to nationalize this issue. I'm sick of going state by state. New York is the media center of the country. It's the immigrant center of the country. It's also a very liberal, Democratic city."

"If he can make it there, in other words, he can make it anywhere," quipped Weintraub in his column, which appeared a few days later.[1]

THE STATUS QUO

Unz concentrated his efforts on New York City, rather than the entire state, because approximately 75 percent of the children identified as limited English proficient in the state of New York were living in that city's five boroughs. The New York City political leaders, like the ones in California and Arizona, were reluctant to embrace Unz's movement due to the powerful special interest groups favoring bilingual education and the usual fear of losing the fast-growing Latino vote.

Mayor Rudy Giuliani agreed somewhat with the initiatives, but decided against supporting Unz's cause. He was well aware that New York was different from Arizona and California in major ways:

- New York did not allow citizens to put initiatives on its state ballot. This could be done only by the state legislature and required thirty thousand signatures. However, even with the signatures, the New York Board of Education could refuse to accept the initiative. Unz's only remaining option would be to sue either New York City or the state.
- There was no organized group working to dismantle bilingual education in New York.
- In 1974 the New York City Board of Education had entered into a federal consent decree with Aspira, a Hispanic education advocacy group. This decree required the city schools to teach students with Hispanic surnames in their native language. Until 1996, when a group of Latino parents brought forth a lawsuit to challenge this practice, even fourth-generation American children who spoke only English were assigned to a bilingual program if they had a Hispanic surname.[2]

In 2000, according to the New York City Board of Education, nearly 160,000 out of the 1.1 million students in New York City schools were classified as LEP students. About 51 percent of them were enrolled in transitional bilingual education classrooms and were therefore taught most of their school subjects in their native language. Eighty-five percent of the bilingual students spoke Spanish, a language many teachers knew at a basic level. Few teachers had any knowledge of the 144 other languages and dialects spoken by LEP students. Generally, ELLs who spoke languages other than Spanish were put in English as second language classes, where they were taught mostly in English.

In 2000 Giuliani appointed a mayoral task force on bilingual education that made a comparison between bilingual education and ESL by tracking the longitudinal academic progress of LEP students between 1991 and 1999. Of the children in bilingual classrooms, 73 percent of the children who began as kindergartners, 62 percent as first graders, 42 percent as second graders, and 44 percent as third graders had transferred into mainstream classrooms within the state-mandated three years. The ESL students had done considerably better, with 84 percent of those who entered as kindergartners, 80 percent as first graders, 76 percent as second-graders, and 70 percent as third-graders making the three-year cutoff.[3] Clearly, the most rapid English learning was made by ESL students who had started as early as kindergarten or first grade.

The study looked at the citywide math and reading test scores of both groups and found that the LEP students who had transitioned out of bilingual or ESL instruction within three years performed better in both reading and math than those who stayed in the programs longer.[4]

The task force study found that LEP children who switched back and forth from ESL to bilingual were the worst off.[5] Professor Joseph Guzman's study would reach the same conclusion in 2002 (see introduction, p. xxvi).

A PLAN FOR IMPROVEMENT

Giuliani would have preferred paring down the bureaucracy by moving LEP students into the mainstream sooner—possibly in two years. Former assistant US secretary of education Diane Ravitch agreed that the push should be to teach children English: "Surely in that budget of $11 billion, they [New York City Board of Education members] should be able to eke out the money to teach everyone the language that's commonly used in most parts of this society."[6]

New York City civic leaders sought to find their own solutions within the Aspira consent decree in order to avoid the dissension that had resulted from the citizens' initiatives in California and Arizona. On February 28, 2001, the seven-member New York City Board of Education approved—unanimously, as a compromise—a $75 million plan for students now designated English language learners. The plan, which would expand parental choice, but not defy the Aspira consent decree, included the following:

- Parents would be able to choose among several programs, including English immersion.
- New intense English immersion programs would be created for sixth graders and beyond.
- More qualified bilingual teachers would be hired for more dual language programs.

Ron Unz objected to the board's decision because the Hispanic ELLs would still be put into bilingual education classes unless their parents insisted they be transferred to ESL programs. Unz complained, "Faced with pressure from bilingual activists to do nothing and pressure from the media to do something, the conflicted leaders of New York schools have decided to do nothing but call it something."[7]

PROGRAM UNDERFUNDED

In July 2001, New York City schools chancellor Harold Levy admitted that the city could not come up with $19.5 million, the city's portion of the $75 million required for the new programs. The plan would have to be scaled back: Each district would have only one intensive English program, five dual language academies would be created instead of twenty, and no new teachers would be hired and trained.[8]

The *New York Daily News* had not agreed with the new plan in the first place. In an editorial, it recommended that the chancellor "should be fighting to eliminate the $169 million sham of a program and take the lead in making sure New York City school children are educated in English. And that they learn it well. Their very futures are at stake."[9]

BLOOMBERG'S REVERSAL

During the fall 2001 election to replace the termed-out Guiliani for New York City mayor, Democratic candidate Mark Green insisted that the city needed to spend more money on hiring bilingual teachers. He was addressing the fact that many bilingual education teachers were uncertified, and some were weak in English. Michael Bloomberg, the Republican candidate, stated that there were more pressing needs and that the first priority should be teaching children English.[10] Very likely Bloomberg had seen the polls indicating that New Yorkers favored English immersion over bilingual education.

Thus bilingual education became one of the candidates' main issues—with Bloomberg seeming to oppose it until he was elected on November 6, 2001, with 49 percent to Green's 47 percent of the vote, and then everything changed. In June 2003, just eighteen months after taking office, Bloomberg agreed to expand the city's bilingual education programs by spending an additional $20 million for students to take core courses in their native languages.

As much as Unz wanted to do something about New York City's flawed bilingual education programs, he was wise to take his movement elsewhere.

SMALL GAINS, WITH ROOM FOR IMPROVEMENT

In 2003 New York City mayor Michael Bloomberg and schools chancellor Joel Klein launched its Children First reform program for ELLs. The reforms included the following: (1) alignment of ELL programs to new standards; (2) improving instruction; (3) implementing effective assessments; (4) holding schools accountable; and (5) increasing parental participation.[11] This fit well with the federal mandates based on the No Child Left Behind Act of 2001.

In 2009 the study *Diverse Learners on the Road to Success*, conducted by the Office of English Language Learners of the New York City Department of Education, examined the progress of the ELL reforms from 2003 through 2008. It presented the following data:

- The percentage of ELLs who scored proficient on the New York State English as a Second Language Achievement Test improved every year, from 3.7 percent in 2003 to 13.4 percent in 2008.
- As a group, Spanish-speaking ELLs, who now made up 68 percent of total ELLs, continued to register the lowest achievement. Only about 26 percent reached proficiency by the fourth grade, compared to 46 percent of Chinese speakers, 50 percent of Korean language speakers, and 34 percent of Russian speakers. Only the speakers of Haitian Creole had a lower percentage rate, at 25.3.
- Hispanics were by far the group most likely to become "long-term" ELLs—that is, students who continued to participate in ELL programs for six years or longer. They made up about 84 percent of all long-term ELLs in 2008. That figure dropped slightly, to 80.3 percent in 2015.[12]

Spanish-speaking students in New York City have always been the language group overwhelmingly enrolled in bilingual education programs. They are also the ones most likely to have teachers who speak their first language to them, even in ESL classes.

It is important to note that ESL is not the same as sheltered or structured English immersion instruction, which was required in the English for the Children initiatives. Generally, SEI instruction is more rigorous than ESL in the teaching of the structure and vocabulary of the English language. SEI teachers are restricted from using the students' home language beyond an occasional direction or clarification of a concept. ESL teachers may speak the home language throughout the lessons and sometimes are even encouraged to do so.

The 2009 report made no mention regarding the success of bilingual versus ESL instruction, nor about the percentage of ELL students in each program. However, bilingual education was on the decline. The New York City Department of Education reported that by 2015 only 17 percent of ELLs were formally in bilingual education classes.

Whether the program is ESL, SEI, or bilingual education, the goal should always be to move students as soon as possible into mainstream classrooms where the more challenging, interesting teaching goes on, and where there is daily contact with English speakers. Growing evidence reveals that children who gain English proficiency at an early age—ideally, in prekindergarten or kindergarten—and in the shortest amount of time become the most success-ful in academics throughout their schooling. Unfortunately, since 2015 this has not been a high priority in New York City public schools.

Because Hispanics have remained the dominant group needing language services, often longer than six of their school years (not counting preschool and kindergarten), New York City school officials should be asking the following questions:

- Do teachers speak Spanish to them? If so, to what degree and for what purpose?
- Do these students have the opportunity to spend at least some of their time in mainstream classes? If so, in which classes and for how long?
- Have school officials identified the students whose deficiencies center around literacy rather than English language acquisition? If so, are they providing them remedial instruction in reading and writing, rather than wasting their time on repetitive language drills?
- Do the families of these children tend to be transient? If so, what is the New York City schools chancellor doing to make sure the curriculum for them is aligned and consistent throughout the boroughs and with other school districts throughout the state?
- Are classroom teachers consciously providing positive support to encourage these students to perform their best on the high-stakes English proficiency tests and to lessen their anxiety over moving from a comfortable ELL environment to the challenges of the mainstream?

There is no data available presently that answers these questions. Yet Chancellor Carmen Fariña of the New York City Department of Education is enlarging the number of bilingual programs. This will most certainly delay both English language acquisition and the entry of Spanish-speaking students into mainstream classrooms.

ELLs in transitional bilingual or dual-language programs receive instruction in English for only 10 to 35 percent of academic class time in kindergarten through third grade. After several years, as the percentage of their instruction in English increases to 60 percent in fourth grade and beyond, transitional students are expected to be able to enter the English-speaking mainstream well prepared. Unfortunately, that is more a pipe dream than a reality for most of these children. The dual language students remain sequestered indefinitely because the purpose of this program is for both the ELLs and native English speakers to end up totally bilingual.

DUAL-LANGUAGE AND TRANSITIONAL BILINGUAL PROGRAMS SURGE

In time for the 2015–2016 school year, Fariña, who was appointed by Mayor Bill DeBlasio in 2013, expanded the number of dual language programs from 150 to 190 in elementary, middle, and high schools in all five of the city's boroughs. There is no indication in her press release that she presented data of any sort to justify this increase. The federal government provided $1 million in federal funds for this project, and each of the fifteen new Model Dual Language Programs received an additional $10,000 for instructional materials.[13]

A majority of the dual-language schools decided to offer Spanish; others offered Japanese, Hebrew, Chinese, French, and Haitian Creole. School officials hoped these programs would attract more middle-class families to schools in impoverished neighborhoods. According to Kate Menken, associate professor of linguistics at the City University of New York, the parents "see dual immersion as an alternative to gifted and talented programs."[14] It appears that the New York City Department of Education has been bending to the will of the middle class at the expense of Spanish-speaking children from mostly low-income families.

The following year, on April 4, 2016, Fariña, announced that an additional thirty-eight bilingual programs would be implemented for the 2016–2017 school year: twenty-nine of them dual language and nine of them transitional bilingual education. Again, she cited no data to justify her decision. Instead, Fariña praised the new programs: "As a former English language learner, I know that a strong education makes all the difference, and these new bilingual programs will give students the foundation to succeed in the classroom and beyond."[15]

The implementation of these programs was reported to cost $980,000 and would be funded by federal Title III. The chancellor made it clear that the New York City Division of English Language Learners and Student Support of the Department of Education intended to expand the bilingual education offerings each year thereafter.[16]

On February 28, 2017, for the third consecutive year, Fariña announced the implementation of still more bilingual programs: thirty-nine dual language and twenty-nine transitional bilingual ones, scheduled to open in September 2017. She asserted, "We've made essential strides for ELL and bilingual students, and these rigorous programs will establish a path to long-term student success while bringing parents to the classroom in new ways."[17] Her comment regarding parents referred to the expansion of translation and interpretation services.

The chancellor did not elaborate on what she meant by "rigorous programs" nor "essential strides." She did not set any goals or commit to specific achievement outcomes; instead, she repeatedly expressed in hyperbolic language that these programs would result in increased bilingualism and higher achievement. It appeared that Fariña's office had not made the effort to analyze how these programs would affect the English language development of ELLs, the students for whom these programs were actually created and funded.

According to her biography, as the daughter of refugees from Spain, Fariña learned English as the sole Spanish speaker in her Brooklyn kindergarten in the late 1940s. This was in the ideal setting at an ideal age for her to become fluent in English. The following year she entered the mainstream— and most likely did well.

While continuing her education in New York City public schools, like many immigrant children of that period, the chancellor's proficiency in English developed at such a rate that she excelled in academics, eventually earning master's degrees from Brooklyn College, Fordham University, and Pace University. She maintained her first language, one assumes, because she continued to speak Spanish in her home.

It is difficult to understand Fariña's fondness for bilingual education considering its poor record in New York City schools and the fact that the chancellor was not educated in any such program herself. However, immersion expert Rosalie Pedalino Porter has noted, "It has been my experience, in panel discussions of educators, dozens of times and in dozens of university settings across the country, that the academics and graduate students who argue most fiercely in favor of bilingual education for ELLs are uniformly people who have never themselves ever been enrolled in bilingual classrooms."[18]

If early fluency and literacy in English are the urgent goals of school programs for ELLs, then all data indicate that an early focus on this target language is the most desirable path. This does not mean ELLs entering preschool and the early grades do not need extra help. The most effective programs provide a structured curriculum that teaches the English language and subject matter concurrently, rather than teaching in the child's native language for part of the school day, then translating into English for the remainder of the day.

New York City Department of Education officials have not compared the achievement of ESL students to those in bilingual programs since the Giuliani task force study in 2000. Instead, they have contrasted the ELL students in every other imaginable way: ethnic background, family income, types of disabilities, school interruptions, length of time in the country, and so on. Most likely, they fear results similar to those of Giuliani's group seventeen years ago: that they will find that students learn English best by being taught in English.

STATISTICS FOR THE STATE OF NEW YORK

According to the US Department of Education, between the 2007–2008 and 2014–2015 school years, the average rate for yearly reclassification and entry into mainstream classrooms in the state of New York was only 16 percent. During the same period, monitored former limited English proficient students reached proficiency in math, on average, at a rate of 57.8 percent, compared to 71 percent for all students in New York. They reached proficiency in reading, on average, at a rate of 46.8 percent, compared to all students at 65.1 percent.[19] Increasing bilingual education will only make this tragic situation worse.

CHARTER SCHOOL ALTERNATIVES

New York City charter schools offer an alternative for the parents of ELLs who want better outcomes for their children than are possible in the district schools. According to a Manhattan Institute study, ELLs in charter schools are more likely to attain proficiency in English on the New York State English as a Second Language Achievement Test (NYSELAT) and become declassified as "former ELLs" at a faster rate than their district counterparts.[20] In addition, according to empirical research, New York City charter students in general perform better than they would have in district schools.[21] Unfortunately, many of these charter schools have waiting lists that postpone—sometimes indefinitely—ELLs' entry into them.

The percentage of online charter school applicants self-identifying as ELLs in New York City increased from 7.4 percent in 2015 to 26.1 percent in 2017. The rise in ELLs' charter school participation may explain to some degree why the total number of New York City ELLs decreased, from about 160,000 in 2000 to 151,000 in 2015. The shift of ELLs from district to charter schools will likely continue at even higher rates because of New York City schools chancellor Carmen Fariña's efforts to continually create and expand bilingual education programs.

Chapter Eight

Colorado's Missed Opportunity

On Wednesday, June 4, 1998, one day after Proposition 227 passed in California, about seventy Hispanic activists, parents, children, and other interested Coloradoans rallied at the State Capitol Building in Denver. They were there to oppose California's English for the Children movement, fearing that Ron Unz might initiate an anti–bilingual education amendment to their state constitution, the only way education policy can be altered in Colorado. They were correct to be concerned, because the polls in Colorado showed that a majority of Latinos wanted to end bilingual education for limited English proficient students.

D. J. Ida, director of child and adolescent services for the Asian Pacific Development Center, lamented, "Our children deserve no less than anybody else. What you do is start with the children's strengths. We blame bilingual education programs when we don't even give them the proper resources."[1]

At the time, parents and school officials in the Denver Public Schools (DPS), the largest school district in the state, were debating the issue. DPS served more than 80,000 students, of which about 13,700 were limited English proficient. The Spanish-speaking English language learners, who comprised 87 percent of the total, remained in bilingual classes for an average of five years, with the district negotiating with federal authorities to reduce the time to three years.

A *Rocky Mountain News* editorial criticized the backers of bilingual education for refusing to admit there was any need for reform. The newspaper did not want a Colorado version of California's Prop 227, but reflected on the reason for the process: "to function as a safety valve for citizen frustration when the civic elite simply refuses to respond to grass-roots pressure."[2]

The editorial scolded President Bill Clinton's administrative officials for saying that maybe bilingual education should be limited to three years but then opposing the US House committee's vote on a three-year limit. The newspaper also chided Clinton's officials for not accepting the modest reform the DPS had requested months earlier.[3]

THE COMPROMISE

Ten months before Prop 227's passage, on July 31, 1997, the Office for Civil Rights of the US Department of Education served DPS superintendent Irv Moskowitz notice, with a twenty-two-page letter, that DPS was failing its LEP students. The OCR was responding to a complaint from the Denver parent group Padres Unidos, an organization supported by the National Council of La Raza. The letter stated that DPS had discriminated against LEP students by not providing them with services they needed to get a proper education:

- DPS had not hired enough qualified teachers.
- LEP students had not been provided with adequate instructional materials.
- Some LEP students had been wrongly classified as special education students.
- The district lacked an effective transition from a language program to the mainstream.
- There had been no follow-up on the progress of former LEP students after they were placed in mainstream classrooms.[4]

In late September 1997, DPS superintendent Moskowitz and Denver Board of Education member Rita Montero, who believed DPS was keeping LEP children too long in bilingual education, took their first of many trips to Washington, DC, to work out a compromise with the federal government. Denver school officials wanted to use multiple measures of achievement to place students into the mainstream, more freedom to waive students from language programs, and more time to train teachers. The OCR insisted on maintaining the requirement that students could not exit the program until they had performed at the 30th percentile on a standardized, nationally normed test. At stake was $30 million in federal school funding.

DPS officials followed up with a revised plan, with the goal of gradually transitioning LEP students into mainstream classrooms within three years. This would allow more time for those who needed it and faster access to the mainstream for those who were ready. There would be frequent evaluations, even of those students who had moved completely into mainstream classes.

Finally, in February 1999, eighteen months after the delivery of the OCR complaint, the US Department of Justice, which had taken over the case, approved the three-year-limit approach that DPS had asked for. It had cost the Denver schools more than $100,000 in lawyers' fees and travel expenses to reach an agreement that included the following:

- Instead of sole reliance on standardized test scores to determine exit out of bilingual education, a team of teachers and administrators would consider other measures of academic progress.
- All of the district's four thousand teachers would be provided extensive training in bilingual education.
- School officials would have the authority to exempt some students from the goal of mainstreaming in three years.

As expected, there was opposition from the activists. Ramon Del Castillo, cochair of Denver's Latino Education Coalition compared limiting bilingual education to what happened with the Native Americans, calling it "cultural genocide."[5] Roberto Cruz of the National Hispanic University in San José, California, said, "If you want to destroy a people, take away the language, because the culture will follow."[6]

Supporters had their say as well. Parent Lorraine Dominguez noted that her son was getting so confused between Spanish and English that he was making up his own words, so she moved him into an English-only class.[7] Others complained that the main reason test scores among Hispanics were so low was that the students had languished in bilingual classes too long. Regardless, the issue appeared to be resolved. Both sides were getting something out of the agreement.

THE $3.3 MILLION BILINGUAL EDUCATION GRANT

A year after the resolution agreement, in March 2000, newly hired DPS superintendent Sidney "Chip" Zullinger submitted a bilingual education grant proposal to the US Department of Education. Acting independently of the Denver school board, Zullinger worked with the Latino/Latina Research & Policy Center at the University of Colorado Denver and the federally funded BUENO Center for Multicultural Education at the University of Colorado Boulder to create a $3.3 million draft proposal that included:

- $1 million for office space and bilingual education teachers' salaries;
- a full-time program director to be paid a salary of $66,000 for the first year, increasing gradually to $75,737 after the fifth year, with more than $85,000 over the life the grant for fringe benefits, including health, dental, and life insurance;
- $10,000 for each of the five years in which ten teachers and staff members would attend the National Association of Bilingual Educators

conferences;
- $104,000 for forty bilingual education teachers to study in Mexico for a week; and
- the remainder of the $3.3 million to be paid for additional salaries, office supplies, and instructional materials.[8]

The Denver school board fired Zullinger two months later for making decisions without consulting them. The board president called it "a mutually-agreed-upon parting of the ways." Zullinger would continue to receive his $140,000-per-year salary for eighteen months, as his contract required.[9]

But amazingly, after the commotion over Zullinger's independent action, four of the seven board members approved the grant! They allowed Spanish-language literacy as an optional enrichment plan beyond the three-year limit, and bilingual education training would be included in the arrangement as an addition, not as a replacement for DPS district training.

Denver board member James Mejia defended the new program: "Here we have an opportunity to work with a community that has been disengaged from the district for a long time. The direction we're headed in now is to provide more options for teachers, parents and students in the district and this grant will be an additional option."[10]

In August 2000, Montero, who was no longer on the board, and teacher Joseph C'de Baca, formerly a supporter but now a critic of bilingual education, joined together to ask lawyers to file an injunction to postpone the grant program. They insisted that it was not compatible with the district's plan approved by the US Department of Justice.

C'de Baca explained, "Bilingual education has always been a cash cow. These programs take on a life of their own, and as long as bilingual programs are perpetuated, there will need to be more money for more bilingual teachers, more training and a bureaucracy to support it."[11]

C'de Baca's argument had merit. A federal grant stipulates that a school district must enroll a certain number of students in the new program and maintain that enrollment in order for the program to continue. Without that, the grant money dries up. Thus it becomes imperative that school officials convince parents to enroll their children in the program and keep their children there for the sake of maintaining what C'de Baca called "a cash cow."

THE TANCREDO-CHAVEZ BALLOT MEASURE

In April 2000, while the dispute regarding the $3.3 million grant was waging, US Representative Tom Tancredo and Linda Chavez, president of the Center for Equal Opportunity in Washington, DC, decided to create an English-immersion amendment to the Colorado constitution. This ballot measure was similar to the Unz initiatives, but tougher: it offered no waivers, whereas the Unz initiatives allowed three.

In June 2000, C'de Baca became a leader of the Tancredo-Chavez movement. He expressed to the media his reason for opposing bilingual education: "I'd have these kids from Mexico that I knew from Hamilton Middle School when they were in sixth grade, and they were nice kids, good kids. Then I'd see them a few years later at West High School, where I also taught, and they're still in the bilingual program. And they're in 12th grade. And I'd say, 'What the hell is going on here?' Because now they're bi-illiterate."[12]

The Tancredo-Chavez ballot proposal was rejected in July 2000. The Colorado Supreme Court found the wording of the measure to be "unclear and misleading."[13] Justice Gregory Hobbs said that the ballot title had failed to mention the provision that no schools shall be required to offer bilingual programs and that the phrase that children must be taught "as rapidly and effectively as possible" would cause confusion.[14]

UNZ AND MONTERO'S BALLOT AMENDMENT

On Wednesday, June 20, 2001, less than one year after the Tancredo-Chavez measure was rejected, Rita Montero began her campaign to formally replace bilingual with sheltered or structured English immersion. She and Jeanine Chavez filed two citizen-initiated amendments to the Colorado Constitution, one of which, if approved, would go before the voters in November 2002. With Ron Unz standing by her side at the State Capitol, Montero explained that she had turned liberal activist after not being able to get her son out of a Denver bilingual program.

Montero described bilingual education as "a program with great intentions that went far astray" and had been taken over by radicals of "the last bastion of the Chicano movement." She accused bilingual educators of exploiting Hispanic children to perpetuate their jobs.[15]

On November 30, 2001, former school board member Laura Lefkowits gave her support to Montero's proposal: "We spent years of our lives trying to reform that entrenched system of Spanish-almost-only classes, yet once we left the Board, everything went back to business as usual, despite clear legal agreements to the contrary. There have been repeated violations of the Bilingual Plan throughout the execution of our newly reformed program."[16]

Lynn Coleman, another former board member, agreed with what Lefkowits had said, adding, "The English for the Children initiative is the only hope for changing things."[17]

On December 5, 2001, a three-member review panel approved the two amendments Montero had submitted, of which one was chosen for the ballot. In opposition, Gully Stanford, cochair of English Plus and chairman of the

Colorado State Board of Education, said he would file a petition for a rehearing, and, should that fail, challenge the measure before the Colorado Supreme Court. He stated, "This is the wrong solution in the wrong place at the wrong time. Everyone in our coalition believes that English must be taught and learned, but this constitutional amendment almost assures it cannot."[18]

In July 2002 the polls showed that 80 percent of voters supported the measure. It appeared that the Colorado amendment would have the same success as the similar California and Arizona initiatives. But that soon changed.

THE DEMISE OF AMENDMENT 31

In August 2002 the Colorado Supreme Court ruled that the measure could be placed on the ballot as Amendment 31. Members of English Plus immediately began working hard to defeat it, renaming their movement "No-on-31."

Stanford shared leadership of No-on-31 with Beverly Ausfahl, former president of the Colorado Education Association, an affiliate of the National Education Association, the largest teachers' union in the United States. The consultant firm of Welchert and Britz agreed to run the campaign. This consultant group had taken down voucher initiatives in Colorado and helped elect Federico Peña as the first Latino mayor of Denver.

The No-on-31 members decided to pursue the issue beyond Denver to all Coloradoans. They said the measure would likely affect virtually every school district except Denver, which was still under a federal court order. There was some truth to their statement, but—as had happened in San José, California—there would be efforts made to consolidate the court order with an amendment approved by the people. After a few years, the amendment would likely prevail.

No-on-31 focused on what the group claimed to be the unintended consequences of the measure:

* Parental involvement and choice would be eliminated.
* The measure allowed for too much litigation, especially against teachers.
* The cost to the taxpayers would "skyrocket,"[19] based on a provision of the amendment that appropriated $5 million per year for ten years toward English tutoring.

No-on-31 took their message to rural, suburban, and urban Colorado communities. The group was able to convince the state's popular Republican governor, Bill Owens, into opposing the measure because of its punitive provisions.

Like Props 227 and 203, Amendment 31 would punish any district employee or school board member for "willfully and repeatedly" refusing to implement the terms of the waiver section. Violators would not only be removed from office but also "barred from holding any position of authority anywhere within the Colorado government or the public school system for a subsequent period of five years."[20]

However, Amendment 31 went beyond the California and Arizona measures regarding the rights of the parents of ELLs: "Parents who apply for and are granted exception waivers . . . still retain for ten years thereafter the full legal right to sue the individuals who granted such waivers if they subsequently conclude during that period that the waivers were granted in error and ultimately injured the education of their child."[21]

Those issues, combined with a single generous contribution to No-on-31, made the difference. In late September, heiress and parent Pat Stryker, a resident of Fort Collins, Colorado, bought $3 million worth of TV time to defeat Amendment 31. She was concerned that Amendment 31 put in jeopardy the dual-language program in which her child participated.

Amendment 31 did not allow Spanish-speaking students to partake in dual-language programs as long as they were classified as LEP students, now referred to as English language learners. Thus, if the measure passed, the schools could not justify using state and federal funds meant for ELLs for dual-language classes, and the dual-language programs would end unless other funding sources were made available.

Because of Stryker's huge contribution, No-on-31 had the means to create a television ad referred to as "Chaos in the Classroom," which ran several times every day on mainstream Colorado television stations. With dramatically morbid music playing in the background, images of little children, who looked Hispanic, appeared on the screen with a dire warning from a voice, "Amendment 31 will knowingly force children who can barely speak English into regular classrooms, creating chaos and disrupting learning."[22]

The *Rocky Mountain News'* "Ad Watch" called the ad "inexcusable."[23] The *Wall Street Journal* asked, "Where are the La Raza, MALDEF and the other self-styled Hispanic lobbies in response to this demagoguery? They don't seem to mind anti-immigrant innuendo as long as it helps preserve bilingual ed booty."[24] Nevertheless, the ad and the ten-year litigation parental provision worked.

DEFEAT

On November 5, 2002, Colorado voters defeated Amendment 31 by a margin of 56 to 44 percent. According to the publication *Breaking the Code*, Ron Unz was the sole contributor to the Amendment 31 campaign, donating approximately $350,000. Contributions from between eight hundred and one thousand different individuals and organizations, in addition to Stryker's $3.3 million, had provided ample funding for the defeat of the measure.[25]

A SURGE IN ELL ENROLLMENT

The Colorado Department of Education reported that between the school years 2008–2009 and 2015–2016 the state's total K–12 enrollment increased 9.3 percent, to 899,112 students. In contrast, the total number of Colorado's ELLs in federal Title III programs increased more than 24 percent, from 82,432 to 101,228 students. The latter number does not include fluent proficient ELLs and students whose parents refused services; if they were included, the number of ELLs enrolled in the 2015–2016 school year would be 127,189.[26]

About 91 percent of ELLs in Colorado who were receiving federal services in 2015–2016 were in English as a second language classes, with 9 percent in dual-language and transitional bilingual education programs. This does not include 22,432 former ELLs who continued in bilingual education although they qualified for entry into mainstream classes. Approximately 12 percent of the entire ELL population received their language services, mostly ESL instruction, from charter schools throughout the state.

DENVER PUBLIC SCHOOLS SEE THE LARGEST INCREASE

The greatest ELL growth occurred in the state's largest school district, Denver Public Schools. From 1998 to 2012, the district's total number of ELLs had more than doubled, increasing from 13,700 to approximately 30,000 students. By the 2015–2016 school year, 40,826 students—45 percent of all students—were identified as ELLs, with 85 percent having identified Spanish as their home language.[27]

With such a surge in the ELL population, the DPS administrators had become overwhelmed with trying to educate so many students with language needs while abiding by its agreements with BUENO, Padres Unidos, and others connected with the federal government. They continued to offer a choice of programs: dual language, TBE, or ESL.

The number of dual-language schools in DPS decreased from 6 schools in 2015 to 3 schools two years later, a very small number in a district of 207 schools. Two dual-language schools had to close because of the poor academic performance of both the Spanish-speaking ELLs and the English-dominant students, who had been learning together in both languages.

The majority of ELLs in Colorado schools have been enrolled solely in ESL classes, which has not been the case in the Denver schools, according to

DPS data. During the 2017–2018 school year, a total of 23,335 elementary ELLs were eligible for federal Title III services: 52 percent of them participated in TBE in fifty-two schools; 42 percent, in some form of ESL instruction in thirty-nine schools; fewer than 1 percent, in three dual-language schools; and 4 percent, not in any programs in five schools. Thus, 978 ELLs were not enrolled in any federal program, due either to a shortage of teachers qualified to instruct ELLs or to parental refusal.

TRANSITIONAL BILINGUAL EDUCATION IN DENVER SCHOOLS

The Denver Public Schools Language Allocation Guidelines explains the district's TBE program,[28] highlighting the Thomas and Collier study as justification for the program. (See introduction, p. xxiv, for a critical analysis of this study.) ELL students enrolled in TBE in the Denver schools receive a limited amount of English instruction in the early grades. That percentage increases as the TBE students advance through the grades (see table 8.1).

This schedule contradicts the evidence that shows children identified as ELLs who have gained English proficiency through immersion in preschool, kindergarten, and/or first grade have excelled academically from that point forward at a much greater rate than those who were not fully exposed to English at an early age.

DEALING WITH FEDERAL AUTHORITIES

During the ELL population growth surge in the Denver Public Schools, serving the linguistic needs of so many ELL students became a challenge. In 2012 a federal judge ordered the DPS to provide at least one forty-five-minute specialized class each day to help students with low English language scores catch up.

Several months later, an insider at the DPS provided the court with internal school records that identified thousands of ELLs—mostly Hispanic stu-

Table 8.1. Estimated Yearly Percentage of Instruction in English

Kindergarten	10 percent
First Grade	30 percent
Second Grade	35 percent
Third Grade	50 percent
Fourth Grade	60 percent
Fifth Grade	60 percent

dents in high schools and charter schools—who had not met the English reading comprehension requirements and had in fact never been enrolled in the mandated classes. The Civil Rights Division of the US Justice Department warned the district several times that every one of the named students needed to be enrolled in an English language acquisition program.[29]

By 2014 the DPS was two years into its latest plan. District administrators at this point had found it impossible to measure the ELLs' achievement for previous years, either because the state assessments had changed or the data had not been tracked.[30] Based on annual testing, one in three of the ELLs who had been in the system for two years had failed to make progress on their English skills. Only 10 percent of all ELLs had become English proficient in 2013.[31] Consequently, the judge ordered the district to extend the court's requirements to the DPS charter schools, increase the number of ELL teachers with proper certification, revise the way students transfer into English classes, and change the way parents pick services.

In 2016, DPS chief schools officer Susana Cordova remarked, "We have an obligation—not just a moral obligation, but a legal obligation—to make sure they [ELLs] are receiving all the services they need. That's something we take very seriously." She explained that the district was still struggling to find the right number of bilingual teachers and multilanguage tutors to deal with students who spoke nearly 180 languages, with Spanish by far the most common.[32]

The commitment to dual language and TBE clashed with the order to improve students' acquisition of English. Cordova should have accepted the fact that it was actually impossible for district schools to make sure the ELLs progressed in English while at the same time teaching the students mostly in Spanish. The main problem had been identified as poor reading comprehension of English, not of Spanish.

Had Amendment 31 passed in 2002, Colorado teachers would have been required to master the techniques of SEI. As a result, the teachers would have learned to instruct ELLs so the students could draw meaning from complex English sentences consisting of twenty or more words. That skill is not transferable from one language to the other and takes a great deal of practice for ELLs to master.

Paul Martinez, the court-appointed DPS monitor, lamented that, according to many educators, some parents follow "former philosophies" that learning English is more important than being bilingual. He stated that the district was now providing more guidance for parents when making their choice.[33] This is reminiscent of earlier instances when Denver school officials coerced parents into enrolling their children in bilingual programs to justify their implementation and continuation.

Martinez entered his fourth status report to the court regarding his findings at the DPS on February 26, 2016. The report stated that none of the identified issues were being ignored by DPS: "They have all been addressed at varying levels or continue to be addressed as part of the district's response to meeting the requirements of the CD [court decree]."[34] According to Martinez, ELL instruction in Denver was finally on the right track.

ASSESSMENTS IN SPANISH

Three weeks earlier, on February 4, 2016, the Colorado State Board of Education received a letter from DPS acting superintendent Susana Cordova, who complained that the state was requiring an interim reading assessment in English for all Colorado students, specifically in grade 3, as Rule 3.04 of the Colorado Reading to Ensure Academic Development (READ) Act. She maintained that assessing ELLs in bilingual classes in Spanish was part of the settlement with the Department of Justice and the Congress of Hispanic Educators, quoting the latest federal consent decree: "The District shall utilize available grade and subject-appropriate reading, writing, math, science, and social studies content assessments in Spanish."[35]

According to Cordova, third grade ELLs in bilingual programs in DPS had consistently scored at higher levels in Spanish than ELLs outside of Denver in English on the assessments for the past four years. It should have been no surprise to anyone that Hispanic ELLs assessed in Spanish, their first language, would score higher in reading than ELLs assessed in English, their second language. Moreover, it is easier to learn to read in Spanish than it is in English because Spanish is considerably more phonetic.

The education board allowed an additional rule to be added to the Colorado READ Act, permitting a school to determine whether an ELL student would take the interim reading assessment in English or the student's native language. Parents could request their children be tested in English, but the schools did not have to honor their request.

In spring 2016, all students were assessed on new standards aligned with Common Core through their yearly state test, the Colorado Measures of Academic Success (CMAS), which was very similar to the nationally developed Partnership for Assessment of Readiness for College and Careers (PARCC). Third and fourth grade ELLs in bilingual programs were eligible to be assessed on the English language arts portion of the CMAS in Spanish. Students in bilingual programs in grades 3–11 were able to take the mathematics, science, and social studies portions of the CMAS in Spanish, as shown in figure 8.1. Former ELLs were permitted general English learner accommodations.

ELL ACHIEVEMENT

The rate of students identified as ELLs in Colorado reaching English language proficiency has been unusually low. Between the school years 2007–2008 and 2014–1015, on average, only 17 percent of all English learners in Colorado, including ELLs not in a program, reached English language proficiency. Colorado ELLs enrolled in federal Title III programs—either ESL or bilingual education—performed considerably worse, with only 12

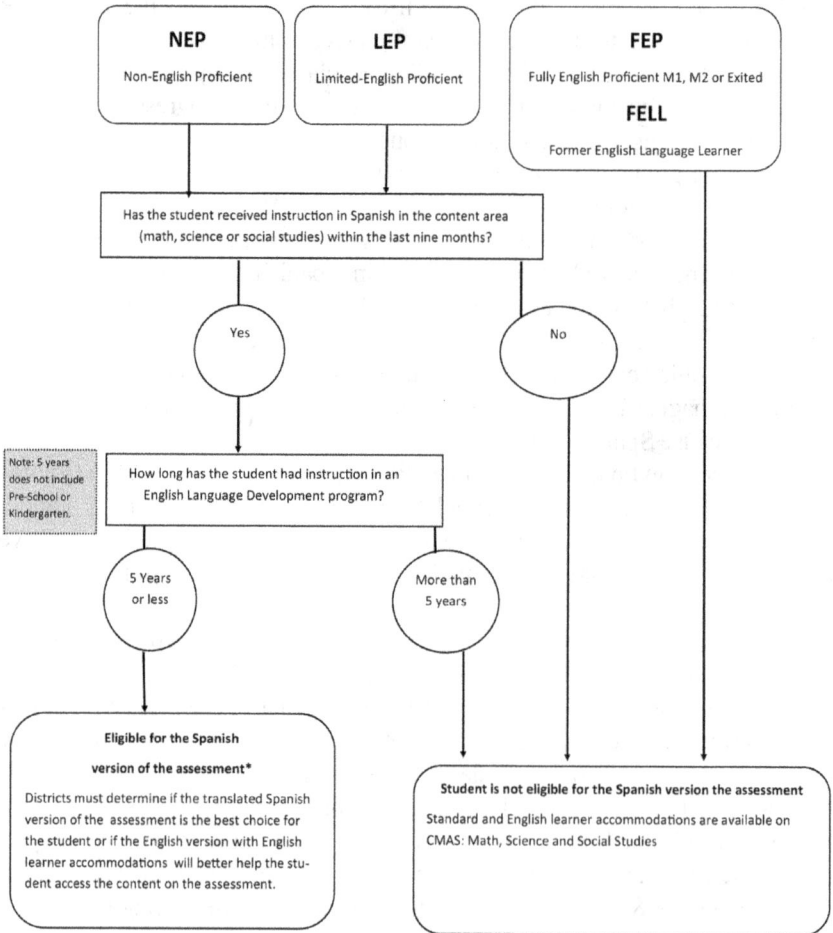

NEP

Non-English Proficient

LEP

Limited-English Proficient

FEP

Fully English Proficient M1, M2 or Exited

FELL

Former English Language Learner

Has the student received instruction in Spanish in the content area (math, science or social studies) within the last nine months?

Yes

No

Note: 5 years does not include Pre-School or Kindergarten.

How long has the student had instruction in an English Language Development program?

5 Years or less

More than 5 years

Eligible for the Spanish version of the assessment*

Districts must determine if the translated Spanish version of the assessment is the best choice for the student or if the English version with English learner accommodations will better help the student access the content on the assessment.

Student is not eligible for the Spanish version the assessment

Standard and English learner accommodations are available on CMAS: Math, Science and Social Studies

* District assessment leadership should collaborate with EL staff to evaluate student eligibility and appropriateness of using the Spanish version of the assessment.

2016- 2017

Figure 8.1.   Decision-Making Flowchart for Use of Spanish Assessments

percent reaching English proficiency, 5 percentage points lower than all English learners.[36] In other words, if the parents' goal was for their children to become proficient in English, they were wise to not put them in a program. ELLs in federal Title III programs in the three states that passed English for the Children initiatives did considerably better than ELLs in Colorado, on average, over the same period (see chap. 2, 6, and 9).

Whereas Colorado shows above average progress with most of its students, the Denver Public Schools, which enroll between 40 and 45 percent of all Colorado ELLs, does not. For example, the third graders in the DPS reached proficiency in reading at a rate of 51 percent between 2008 and 2010, whereas in Colorado overall that rate ranged from 70 to 73 percent, according to "Denver Children's Affairs," a report based on Colorado Department of Education data.[37] In the years between 2011 and 2013, the period in which ELLs were allowed to take the reading test in Spanish, the percentage improved to an average rate of 58.7 percent—better, but still not very good and an inaccurate assessment because ELLs were taking the reading test in their native language rather than in English.

The National Center for Education Statistics shows that 61.1 percent of ELLs in Colorado graduated from high school in 2015, 4 percentage points lower than the national average of 65.1. Unfortunately, a Colorado high school diploma does not mean that the recipient of that certificate is prepared for study at a university or community college—especially if that student has been receiving instruction and taking most of his state tests in a language other than English.

According to the report "Denver Children's Affairs," Colorado Department of Education data shows that, on average, 61 percent of Denver Public School graduates enrolled in state public colleges or universities between 2009 and 2011 were required to take developmental (remedial) classes. In comparison, approximately 39 percent of Colorado graduates overall had to take those courses during those years. More recent data was not available.

Chapter Nine

Massachusetts's Rise and Fall

No one has been more vilified by the bilingual education establishment—and more adored by immersion advocates—than Rosalie Pedalino Porter, a perky, articulate, Italian-born woman who immigrated to the United States as a small child. She experienced the challenge of learning English as a second language at her neighborhood school in Newark, New Jersey, when she was only six years old. Several years after mastering English—and then Spanish—while growing up, she became a bilingual education teacher, but she soon ran into conflicts regarding the Massachusetts mandate that required her to teach limited English proficient students mostly in Spanish.[1]

Porter was director of the Institute for Research in English Acquisition and Development throughout the 1990s and early 2000s. She has lectured, edited manuscripts, and written two books, as well as several articles for national education publications. She has testified in court and before the US Congress as an expert on English immersion education. (See chap. 5, pp. 64–65 for her testimony in the *Flores* lawsuit.)

RON UNZ CONTACTS ROSALIE PEDALINO PORTER

In early 2001 Ron Unz telephoned Porter at her home in Amherst, Massachusetts, to discuss with her the possibility that she lead a movement to place an anti–bilingual education initiative on her state's ballot. As much as she liked the idea of doing something about the transitional bilingual education programs in Massachusetts, she let Unz know that she did not think such a measure could succeed with the voters. She told him, "Ron, the two victories must have unhinged your mind, temporarily. Massachusetts is the most left-liberal state in the known universe, it's where political correctness is an inherited gene; it is the state that passed the first bilingual education law in the country, a place full of true believers in the education establishment and inattentive legislators in the State House—groups that will fight hard against change."[2]

Unz disagreed. He argued that Massachusetts was the best place to act next, after his dramatic successes in the west.[3] He believed in his mission and wanted to take it east.

While most Massachusetts politicians and educators still valued highly the state's TBE law, a few disapproved of it vehemently. By the time Unz set his sights on the state, the groundwork to change the law had already been laid by two maverick politicians: Governor William Weld and State Representative Guy Glodis.

TRANSITIONAL BILINGUAL EDUCATION MANDATED IN MASSACHUSETTS

In 1971, when Massachusetts became the first state to require bilingual education, the amount of time designated for enrollment in the program to learn English was set at three years. However, through a waiver system that was not properly enforced, large numbers of students spent four, five, and six years in native language classrooms. The officials at the state level failed to oversee the waiver process, as well as the requirement that these LEP children be tested annually.[4]

The law required that a certified teacher instruct the LEP children through TBE in school districts where there were twenty or more LEP students of the same native language. Thus students were to be instructed in their first language most of the school day in the early grades, with the percentage of instruction in English increasing each year.

By 1990, language-minority students made up 4 percent of the total US student population and 12 percent of the student population in Massachusetts. In the 1991–1992 school year, 58 percent of the Massachusetts's LEP students spoke Spanish.[5] During the 1993–1994 school year, forty thousand students were officially enrolled in TBE in fifty-one of the Bay State's school districts.[6]

The expense amounted to an extra $1,179 per LEP student during the 1992–1993 school year.[7] In 1994, after twenty-three years of TBE, the Massachusetts Bilingual Education Commission was unable to say whether the mandated program had produced good or bad results.[8] The high cost of a program yet to prove beneficial for students brought the issue to the political forefront.

In January 1995 Governor William Weld proposed the following requirements for improving the education of LEP students:

- parental permission to enroll students in bilingual education;
- English instruction provided for at least one-third of the school day;
- time in a program limited to three years;
- teachers to be fluent in English; and
- oversight controlled by the Board of Education.

When the Joint Committee on Education held a hearing on this proposal in April 1995, hundreds of high school students showed up to protest. Hispanic students clapped enthusiastically in response to Porter's statement in favor of the proposal, but after their teacher translated Porter's words into Spanish, they booed. The Hispanic students spoke before the committee individually, but only in Spanish, while the Asian students explained in English what they did not like about the proposal.

Professor Christine Rossell of Boston University commented on the students' presentations at the hearing: "No one, including the students themselves, acknowledged or even seemed to realize that the programs in which these distinct groups were enrolled bore no resemblance to each other, a fact suggested by the language in which each group testified."[9]

The state House of Representatives defeated Weld's bill in a 124–30 vote. The *Boston Globe* chided the Weld administration for wanting to cut costs at the expense of children.[10]

"THE EMPEROR HAS NO CLOTHES"

In *Bilingual Education in Massachusetts: The Emperor Has No Clothes*, authors Christine Rossell and Keith Baker concluded that schools had mostly ignored the stiff requirements of the 1971 law. Only about half of Massachusetts's LEP students—mostly Spanish speakers—were actually being taught in their own language, as required by law.[11]

Having visited seventy-five bilingual classrooms in Massachusetts and analyzed the data thoroughly, Rossell, with agreement from Baker, made suggestions:

- Native-language instruction should be used minimally and only when the LEP students' English ability is very low.
- The need for native-language instruction may be only for a matter of months.
- Teachers who are familiar with but not fluent in the children's language are better teachers for these children because they will not emphasize native-language maintenance, which is detrimental to the students' academic achievement.

- Students of the same language group should not be placed together in the same classroom because it will delay their development of English. [12]

In an interview with a *Boston Globe* reporter, Rossell explained the importance of mixing LEP students with English speakers: "These programs should be fully integrated into regular schools so that students are exposed to English speakers on the playground, in the cafeterias, the halls, assemblies and other areas before, during and after school."[13] Moreover, she opined that the LEP students should not be taught separately for more than a year.

Education and political leaders did not heed Rossell's advice. Most likely, they understood that her recommendation to assimilate LEP students into the mainstream as rapidly as possible would decrease federal and state funding for everyone involved with bilingual programs. The jobs of everyone—from federal and state coordinators, district program directors, and secretaries to officials, teachers, and teachers' aides—would be at risk and possibly eliminated.

As the recipient of several awards for her thoroughly researched studies, Rossell should have been taken seriously. Professor James Schmidt of Boston University described Rossell as "really precise, careful and rigorous."[14] He recalled how convinced she had been that school desegregation had not caused white flight to the suburbs until the data had proven otherwise, continuing, "She is absolutely un-dogmatic and un-ideological. She is willing to change her own views based on what she has found in her own work."[15]

CONCERN OVER CALIFORNIA VICTORIES

After Ron Unz's win in California in 1998, the people of Massachusetts—like those of Arizona and Colorado—discussed the possibility that Unz might bring his cause to their state. Abigail Thernstrom, a member of the Massachusetts Board of Elementary and Secondary Education who described herself as a longtime friend of Unz, agreed with him: "Kids need to learn English if they are to have decent-paying jobs."[16]

Sandra Alvarado, director of the Latino Parents Association in Boston, objected, saying, "What happened in California is not based on fact, but on personal feelings and fear. The reality is those children will not learn in a year. They will sink or swim. We will not let that happen here."[17]

State Representative Guy Glodis expressed his disdain for bilingual education: "We need to abolish bilingual education as soon as possible. California has taken the lead. Bilingual does not work. . . . We as a state and we as a government have an obligation to help minorities and to help people help themselves. Bilingual does not do that."[18]

The usual arguments in support of bilingual education were offered: Some students need more time; subject matter is best taught in the native language until the students have reached fluency in English; preserving the native language has merit; and many students educated through bilingual programs have ended up with good careers. The arguments on the other side were that the immersion process took less time, so students did not have to be segregated for several years and they were more likely to succeed in academics as well as careers if they became fluent and literate in English as rapidly as possible.

The progress of the bilingual education model in Massachusetts could not be measured because, like other states, LEP students were exempt from taking the standardized tests, in this case, the Iowa Test of Basic Skills. Thus it was not possible to evaluate whether the program was working or not. The *Boston Globe* reported that 58 percent of the 5,582 third graders in bilingual education were excused from taking the reading portion of the Iowa Test in 1998, even though 71 percent of them had attended Massachusetts public schools for at least three years. By comparison, only 2 percent of all special education students were pardoned from taking the test. [19]

In 1999 the Massachusetts Board of Education reversed its policy of exempting LEP students from the Iowa Test and required them to be administered the Massachusetts Comprehensive Assessment System (MCAS). Starting with the tenth graders in 2003, all students would be required to pass the tenth grade MCAS in order to receive a high school diploma.

REFORM BILL IN SENATE

On January 11, 2000, Glodis, now a state senator, appeared at the State House on Beacon Hill in Boston to announce his filing of a bill similar to California Proposition 227. The bill would eliminate bilingual education for Massachusetts's LEP children and allow for a sheltered English immersion approach for up to one year.

Glodis pointed to the high failure rate of bilingual education students on the MCAS for the 1998–1999 school year. [20] Some 47 percent had failed English language arts, 87 percent had failed mathematics, and 91 percent had failed science, technology, and history. [21] [*Note:* Such test scores offer only a limited view of the LEP students' progress unless other factors are considered, such as years in the program and level of English language ability.]

According to Glodis, "Non-English speaking students get little English at home or with their friends. So, if not at school, where will they learn English? We need to give them the tools to succeed, and bilingual education is just not working." [22]

Ron Unz stood next to Glodis at the State House and talked about a recent San José *Mercury-News* report of test scores, which showed students who had spoken little or no English initially were learning more in English immersion classes than the 12 percent of students still in bilingual education. Unz stated, "The children and parents want to be in the mainstream. Why should Massachusetts be any different?"[23]

State Representative Jarrett Barrios had organized a protest to Glodis's presentation, which was made up of about fifty people, mostly members of the Massachusetts Coalition for Bilingual Education. The Coalition was temporary—set up for the election—and separate from the MA Association for Bilingual Education (a longtime nationally affiliated organization). This newly formed group included the Massachusetts Federation of Teachers, the Latino Parents Association, the Massachusetts English Plus Coalition, and the National Coalition of Advocates for Students.

Barrios and others said that bilingual education in the Bay State had not received the proper resources, support, and funding. Supporters mentioned Amigos School, a dual-language (Spanish and English) program in Cambridge where the fourth graders had excelled in both math and English on the MCAS. [*Note:* Unlike most schools with high enrollment of LEP students, Amigos served students of well-educated parents who spoke English in the home and who put much effort into their children's academic progress.]

Barrios explained, "Children must learn English, beautiful English. Transitional bilingual education in all its 28 years has never been fully applied. We've known that for a long time, and we've been looking at the bilingual education debacle."[24]

State Representative Antonio Cabral called Glodis's proposal "anti-immigrant propaganda" and went on to say, "Since I've been here, these bills have come and gone. I'm going to predict this bill will come and go."[25]

Because of efforts by both Barrios and Cabral, Glodis's bill failed in the legislature in 2000, as did a similar second measure in 2001. All the while, reports from the national media were praising the increase in achievement of LEP children in California, crediting California Prop 227 with that success. The atmosphere had become ripe for Unz to bring his movement to the Bay State.

ANNOUNCEMENT OF UNZ BALLOT INITIATIVE

On Tuesday, July 31, 2001, Unz stood at the State House with his Massachusetts leadership group for a press conference to announce his plan for an initiative, modeled after Propositions 227 and 203. He stated, "I believe that the parents and voters of Massachusetts should have the right to decide whether their children should be taught in English or not taught in

English."[26]

The night before, Glodis had tried to reach a last-minute compromise with Cabral, but the talks had fallen apart. Glodis was not at the press conference but said in an interview, "The fact is that bilingual education is an embarrassment and is failing the kids it needs to help. I am confident that when this goes on the ballot, it will receive an even higher percentage of votes than it did in California or Arizona."[27] He gave his full support to the campaign and said that he would help collect the necessary 57,100 signatures as soon as the question had approval at the state attorney general's office.[28]

Both supporters and protesters appeared that day at the State House. Some carried placards and shouted at Unz, "Go back to California!" while others stood firmly with him.

Roger Rice of the Multicultural Education and Training Alliance criticized Unz harshly, saying, "Not only is Unz not an educator, he's not a bilingual educator and he's not a parent. He got a few bucks and ran for governor [of California] and failed, and now it's his whole mission in life to stamp out Spanish."[29]

Barrios explained, "We're in this for the long haul. We don't have a plane back to California. The problem with Ron Unz is he wants to get rid of a one-size-fits-all solution and replace it with another one-size-fits-all solution."[30] Barrios gathered with other legislators, city politicians, and activist groups inside the State House after the press conference to discuss how to oppose the Unz movement.

On September 5, 2001, the Massachusetts Attorney General's Office approved not only Unz's measure but also a ballot initiative written by Barrios. The latter measure offered bilingual education options, but was not pursued.

QUESTION 2 CAMPAIGN

Unz put together an impressive threesome, all fluent in Spanish, whom he had personally chosen to lead the English for the Children of Massachusetts movement: as statewide chair, Cuban-born Harvard Law School graduate Lincoln Tamayo, principal of Chelsea High School in Chelsea, Massachusetts, a heavily immigrant community considered to be among the poorest in the state; and as cochairs, Christine Rossell, whose research had convinced her that immersion instruction was more effective than bilingual education, and Rosalie Pedalino Porter, who decided to join the movement because she "couldn't resist," although initially she doubted that the people of Massachusetts would go along with it.[31]

Tamayo stated, "It never made sense to me, that it's best for a child to learn English by learning all subjects in another language. . . . I've seen what a strong education and an ability to learn English has done for me and my ability to provide for my wife and children, and I want that for every kid who comes here not speaking English."[32] Tamayo had entered school unable to speak English as a small child in Tampa, Florida. He had given up his job as principal because the Chelsea schools' superintendent had forbidden him to participate in the movement. His disgust with the failure he had witnessed of bilingual education in his district made it imperative that he seize the opportunity to do something about it.

On December 4, 2001, the English for the Children of Massachusetts supporters turned in petitions with more than 100,000 signatures, far exceeding the required 57,100. As he had in the other states, Unz had hired professional signature gatherers. Also, volunteers had amassed thousands of signatures. On December 20, 2001, the Massachusetts secretary of state certified the initiative and it became officially Question 2.

Like the other campaigns, the leaders involved themselves in as many public debates and appearances as possible, while Unz helped with the finances. They wrote newspaper articles and gave interviews. Unz provided upgraded technology to ensure their good communication. In addition, Unz subsidized Tamayo for a year to help make up the financial loss he experienced after giving up his job to run the campaign.

Mount Holyoke, Northeastern, Harvard, and Wellesley were among the colleges and universities that provided forums for the ballot measure to be debated. These institutions of higher learning insisted on fair debates in which each side was represented by the same number of speakers and shared identical time restrictions.

Other schools and forums were less fair-minded. Tamayo was refused a place on a Simmons College panel discussing Question 2; he was told he could comment, but only from the audience. At Brandeis University, Porter was the sole speaker in favor of Question 2, opposite five opponents. The dean of the School of Education at the University of Massachusetts Amherst invited Porter to speak but admitted that no one on his faculty was willing to debate her. At the scheduled town hall debate, Porter's would-be opponent canceled her appearance upon learning that Porter had also been invited to speak.[33]

OPPOSITION TO QUESTION 2

The Committee for Fairness to Children and Teachers, the main opposing force to Question 2, was led by lawyer Tim Duncan, a member of Acting Governor Jane Swift's reelection committee and parent of a seven-year-old son in the Amigos dual-language school. Because Amigos relied on funding for LEP children, Duncan feared the school would close if the measure passed.

Many important groups supported the cause of the Committee for Fairness: the deans of eight colleges of education; leaders of both teachers' unions; most Democratic officials, who made up about 90 percent of the state legislature; editorial staffs of most newspapers in the state; and Hispanic advocacy organizations. All urged people to vote against the initiative. In addition, US Senators Edward Kennedy and John Kerry signed a full-page ad in the *Boston Globe* that asked people to vote no on Question 2.[34]

By this time, two years had passed since the deluge of national press reports had celebrated the rise in the California LEP students' Stanford-9 test scores, so its impact on the public had softened. As a result, the opposition was able to insist that smaller class sizes and improved reading instruction were the two main reasons for the increase in achievement, not Prop 227, which had ushered in English immersion.

Furthermore, the opposition in Massachusetts made the case—similar to the one put forth at the same time in Colorado—that the law would be overly punitive to teachers, coining the slogan "Don't sue teachers." However, Question 2 was different from Colorado Amendment 31. Whereas the Colorado initiative allowed parents ten years to sue, the Massachusetts measure required that the parents had to "discover before the child reaches the age of eighteen that the application for waivers was induced by fraud or intentional misrepresentation and injured the education of their child."[35]

SUPPORT FOR QUESTION 2

The *Wall Street Journal* denounced the bilingual education advocates in Massachusetts for their depictions of Ron Unz as "hateful" and "spiteful." In addition, the newspaper chided Gerardo Villacres, director of the Hispanic-American Chamber of Commerce in Boston, for attacking Unz's name, saying that "half of the words in his name says Nazi on it, and that says a lot."[36]

The Unz group had an important politician on their side—Mitt Romney, Republican candidate for Massachusetts governor. His stands on the issues were much like those of his Democratic opponent, Shannon O'Brien—except that he supported Question 2. He spoke firmly:

> Shannon O'Brien is as wrong as wrong can be for not supporting the teaching of our children in English. Bilingual education is a well-intentioned program that became a dismal failure. Currently, we have two school systems in Massachusetts—one for children who speak English and another for non-English speakers. If our children cannot speak English fluently, it robs them of their ability to compete for jobs in today's economy.[37]

Romney was not expected to win the election. In a *Boston Globe*/WBZ-TV poll conducted in late September 2002, O'Brien had 42 percent of the vote, whereas Romney trailed with 36 percent. The undecided vote was at 12 percent, with 2 percent refusing to answer.

In response to the charge that Question 2 would be too punitive to teachers, the initiative's backers noted that no one had sued in either California or Arizona. In addition, both Romney and Glodis said frequently that should Question 2 pass, they would work to create legislation that would protect teachers from being sued.

A BILL TO DISMANTLE THE INITIATIVE PASSES

On August 6, 2002, Acting Governor Jane Swift signed English Opportunities for All, a law originally cosponsored by two state legislators, Robert Antonioni and Peter Harkin, in response to Question 2. It limited the LEP children to two years of bilingual education, strengthened the qualifications of bilingual teachers, and increased funding to school districts. Nevertheless, Glodis did not like it, stating, "This law will not change the status quo. It just demonstrates how out of touch Jane Swift is with the majority of the electorate."[38]

VICTORY

The people of Massachusetts surprised the country on November 5, 2002, when Romney won the gubernatorial election with 50 percent of the vote to O'Brien's 45 percent. Question 2 passed by a huge margin, with 68 to 32 percent of the vote. Romney, who was praised for having campaigned "vigorously" for the initiative,[39] had supported Question 2 in television ads in which he stated, "English is the door to opportunity in America. If our children cannot speak English fluently, it robs them of their ability to compete for jobs."[40]

Not counting Romney's ads, the Question 2 campaign had spent $425,000; the opposition to the measure, $725,000. A large increase in Latino voter turnout occurred in urban districts such as Boston, Worcester, and Chelsea. According to Porter, the districts that had the longest experience with bilingual education voted in favor of Question 2.[41]

RON UNZ'S REFLECTIONS

Three days after the election, in a commentary to his supporters, Ron Unz expressed the following regarding how the Colorado's and Massachusetts's separate campaigns had played out:

Thus, with "the Best Conservative Governor in America" [Colorado governor Bill Owens] essentially quoting the Teddy Kennedy line on bilingual education, with Colorado's multiculturalist Latino activists enthusiastically backing a multi-million-dollar [California] Proposition 187–style advertising campaign ["Chaos in the Classroom"] to defend their programs, and with the most liberal [Massachusetts] voters in America setting record margins in requiring an all-English curriculum from the first day of school, Tuesday's initiative votes followed a strange and ironic path.

Who says that politics in America is never interesting?[42]

The elections in Colorado and Massachusetts on November 5, 2002, were the end of Unz's campaigns to dismantle bilingual education in the United States. Seldom heard from again on the subject of bilingual education, Unz moved on to other projects. However, his English for the Children movement brought light to a serious injustice and has improved education policy, especially in the three states that passed the Unz-sponsored initiatives. At the same time, opposition from those highly invested in bilingual education has persisted.

MASSACHUSETTS'S MIRACLE

By 2005, Massachusetts public schools had earned a reputation for preparing students for colleges and universities better than any other state. Between 2005 and 2015, Massachusetts scored first on six consecutive National Assessment of Educational Progress (NAEP) tests in grades 4 and 8 in both reading and mathematics. Between 2007 and 2015, Massachusetts scored among the top countries in grade 8 in mathematics and science on the Trends in International Mathematics and Science Study (TIMSS) and in reading and science on the Program for International Student Assessment (PISA).

Mainstream academic students were not the only ones to show achievement in Massachusetts. Students attending regional vocational/technical high schools in Massachusetts produced high pass scores in mathematics and English on the MCAS. Former Massachusetts Department of Elementary and Secondary Education associate commissioner Sandra Stotsky explained that the vocational/technical high schools had "an attrition rate that is close to zero, and long waiting lists."[43]

As a result of the state's Education Reform Act of 1993, Massachusetts's education standards were developed to improve the skills of students in major subjects, to be measured by the MCAS. All students are administered these state tests in grades 4, 8, and 10. As noted earlier in this chapter, students are required to pass these tests to graduate. [*Note:* Next Generation MCAS replaced MCAS in 2016, but the Massachusetts Department of Elementary and Secondary Education (DESE) still refers to the state tests as "MCAS."]

Whereas it is usual for a state to develop educational standards as well as assessments that align with those standards, Massachusetts officials proceeded in a direction unheard of in other states. As associate commissioner from 1999 to 2003, Stotsky and members of her department totally revised and strengthened the entire system of teacher licensing in every major subject for all prospective, beginning, and veteran teachers. This was a complicated but necessary undertaking to end the practice of assigning instructors to teach subjects they had not themselves mastered.

ASSESSMENTS FOR TEACHERS OF READING

Stotsky and her associates began with reading, the skill most fundamental to education. Starting with elementary education, they strengthened licensure requirements for elementary, early childhood, and special education teachers of reading and reading specialists after discovering that "the original subject tests for early childhood and special education teachers did not assess any research-based knowledge of beginning reading instruction." To correct this omission, they developed stand-alone tests of reading instructional knowledge: one for the three groups of teachers who teach reading (as well as other subjects) and another at the graduate level for reading specialists (not administrators). [44]

Stotsky went through a long and thorough process that included meetings with educators throughout the state and revisions to her original draft outline that took into consideration suggestions from well-known reading professors. She moved away from sole reliance on the popular whole language theory to requiring knowledge of systematic decoding. The stand-alone Foundations of Reading (90) licensure test became operational in 2002. [45]

There is no doubt that Foundations of Reading (90) had a great deal to do with Massachusetts students' excellent showing on both national and international tests in reading and other subjects within three years. Beginning in 2009, Connecticut, Wisconsin, New Hampshire, Mississippi, and North Carolina adopted this reading test, with a similar cutoff score for passing and few or no changes in content. [46]

As recounted in Stotsky's book *An Empty Curriculum*, since 2001, the licensure requirements for teachers of reading, mathematics, social studies, science, and other subjects have made a difference to all Massachusetts students, including LEPs, often referred to as English language learners. Whether ELL or LEP, the term designates a *temporary* stage of English language development. While students are improving their English skills through SEI, they are taught regular content curricula in modified English. After reaching

English proficiency and entering mainstream classrooms, they receive the same instruction as other students—hopefully from well-prepared teachers, as was Stotsky's intent.

ELL ASSESSMENTS: ACCESS

Federal and state laws require ELLs to be assessed annually in listening, speaking, reading, and writing. In Massachusetts, all students designated ELL, whether in a special program or not, have been required to take Assessing Comprehension and Communication in English State-to-State (ACCESS) annually since the 2012–2013 school year.

Specific accommodations, such as the signing of test directions for deaf children and large-print versions for children with visual problems, are provided for ELLs with documented disabilities. The following actions are not allowed under any circumstance during the administering of ACCESS:

* reading aloud test items on the Reading Test;
* translating test items into a language other than English;
* signing test items, passages, and/or response options (answer choices);
* oral reading of test items in a language other than English;
* student use of bilingual word-to-word dictionaries; and
* student response to test questions in a language other than English.[47]

The purpose of ACCESS is to evaluate students identified as ELLs on their progress in mastering the English language and to identify at what level they should receive instruction to progress further. With accommodations, students with disabilities and/or only a short time of exposure to English can be evaluated in a meaningful way.

STATE ASSESSMENTS: MCAS

Like all Massachusetts public school students, ELLs are required to take the state-mandated high-stakes MCAS, more recently called MCAS 2.0 or Next Generation MCAS. Not only are accommodations provided for students with learning disabilities, but adjustments are also made in consideration of ELLs' actual level of English proficiency.

For beginning ELLs, usually first-year students in the program, the MCAS English language arts section is optional as long as the students have participated in the entire ACCESS. Those students are required to take the MCAS mathematics and technology/engineering portions with accommodations. Beginning ELLs' scores are excluded from school and district summary results; all other ELL results are included.

Beginning ELLs whose English is at the lowest level are allowed to have tests read to them, repeated, and clarified; intermediate and advanced ELLs whose English is fluent in basic conversation but lacking in academic proficiency are permitted to use a bilingual word-to-word dictionary. Table 9.1 explains all accommodations allowed for ELLs while taking the MCAS.

Table 9.1.   Guidance on Selecting Accommodations for English Learners

#	Accommodation	Most Likely to Benefit English Learners at the Following English Proficiency Levels		
		Beginning	Intermediate	Advanced
EL1	Paper-based edition of the grades 3–8 Mathematics or STE tests for a first-year ELL with a low level of English proficiency or who is unfamiliar with technology	◎	○	○
EL2	Approved bilingual word-to-word dictionary and glossary (English/Native Language)	○	●	●
EL3.1 and EL3.2	Text-to-speech or human read-aloud for the Mathematics or Science and Technology/Engineering tests (in English)	●	◎	○
EL4.1 and EL4.2	Human scribe or speech-to-text for Mathematics or STE responses	●	◎	○
EL5	Read aloud/repeat/clarify general administration directions in English (by test administrator)	●	◎	○
EL6	Read aloud/repeat/clarify general administration directions in student's native language (by test administrator)	●	◎	○

KEY for Table 9.1:

● **Highly recommended** for use by English learners at this ELP level
◎ **Recommended** for use by English learners at this ELP level
○ **May not be appropriate** for students at this ELP level

Note: This table provides guidance regarding the suitability of ELL accommodations based on the English language proficiency (ELP) level of the student.

Former ELLs may use authorized word-to-word dictionaries and glossaries when taking the English language arts, mathematics, and science and technology/engineering portions of the MCAS. Dictionaries that include definitions, synonyms, antonyms, phrases, and other information are strictly prohibited.

ELLs enrolled in US schools for fewer than three years are given the option of taking the Spanish edition of the grade 10 MCAS mathematics section if they are literate or at near grade level in Spanish. To graduate, they must pass the English language arts and science and technology/engineering sections in English.

NAEP SCORES

For three years after the passage of Question 2, the students identified as ELLs in Massachusetts improved considerably in reading on the NAEP. On the fourth grade reading assessment, 32 percent of ELLs scored basic or above in 2003; 50 percent scored at that level in 2007. On the eighth grade reading assessment, 24 percent scored at basic or above in 2003; 40 percent scored at that level in 2007.

These scores had declined somewhat by 2015, but they remained higher than in 2003 and still exceeded the scores of ELLs in other states. Forty-four percent of fourth grade ELLs scored basic or above in reading, 12 percentage points above the NAEP national average for ELLs. Thirty-two percent of eight grade ELLs scored basic or above in reading, which was 7 percentage points above the NAEP national average for ELLs. In math, both the fourth grade and eighth grade ELLs scored 7 percentage points above the NAEP national average for ELLs.[48]

Sixty-four percent of ELLs graduated from Massachusetts high schools in 2015, just 1 percentage point below the national average for ELLs. Very likely, this rate would have been higher had it not been for the fact that the tests required for graduation vary considerably among the states—with the challenging MCAS offering only limited accommodations for ELLs.

THE PROFICIENCY GAP TASK FORCE

In 2009 the DESE established the Proficiency Gap Task Force to analyze the situation regarding ELLs and other low-performing student groups. The members agreed that there was a problem with the term *proficiency gap* in that Massachusetts's NAEP reading and math scores on average were at the top both nationally and internationally. Thus the achievement gap was greater than the gap in the other states—not because of the low performance of the

ELLs and other at-risk groups, but because of the high performance of the students overall.

The task force found successes such as at Brockton High School, the largest high school in the state. The students were mostly poor minorities (69 percent), with 14 percent classified as ELLs. Only 27 percent scored proficient or higher on the tenth grade English language arts section of the MCAS in 2000; 79 percent scored that high in 2009. Four other at-risk high schools with smaller numbers of ELLs also showed high achievement. The results offered "undeniable evidence" that children could be moved to the highest standards of achievement, but that the educators had to make it happen.[49]

The task force made recommendations specific to ELLs, including:

- school-centered programs appropriate for the ELLs' age and English proficiency;
- stronger requirements for teachers of ELLs;
- more data-driven monitoring of ELLs at the district level; and
- enrichment of professional development for all educational leaders across the state in relationship to the education of ELLs.

In 2011 the US Department of Justice investigated Massachusetts schools for civil rights violations, claiming that too many ELLs had been placed in classes with inadequately prepared teachers. By then, the ELL population in Massachusetts schools had grown to 68,000. According to the federal investigators, more than 45,000 teachers in 275 school districts across the state needed better training on how to teach ELLs, especially in the content areas. The federal agents stated that current training in Massachusetts was "difficult for teachers to obtain and potentially out of date."[50]

By the end of the 2013–2014 school year, the enrollment of ELLs had increased by 54 percent since the 2003–2004 school year, from 49,297 to 75,947 students, equaling 7.8 percent of the total student population in Massachusetts. By 2017 that figure had reached 9.5 percent. Unfortunately, the schools had been unable to implement the recommendations of the task force for this rapidly growing population.

MASSACHUSETTS ELL PROFILES AND PROGRESS REPORT

In 2015 DESE commissioned the Center for English Language Learners at the American Institutes for Research to provide profiles of Massachusetts ELLs and policy recommendations for improving their outcomes. DESE was concerned that English learners who entered ELL programs in kindergarten and exited after three years were struggling academically after their exit. Another concern was that ELL students were not exiting from the program at all.

In October 2015 the AIR group completed a longitudinal study of ELLs over a period of ten school years, from 2003–2004 to 2013–2014, in ten Massachusetts school districts.[51]

The study included the five districts with the highest concentration of ELLs statewide, ranging from 27 to 35 percent (Worcester, Lawrence, Boston, Holyoke, and Lowell); four districts with students chosen based on concentrations of students from low-income households and growth in English language proficiency (Weymouth, Wachusett, Quincy, and Fall River); and the district with the most innovative programs (Brockton). These districts had experienced large growth in their ELL populations, sometimes more than 50 percent, with the exception of Quincy, where the increase was less than one percent. In eight districts, 49.5 to 96 percent of the student body came from low-income families; the exceptions were Weymouth (30 percent) and Wachusett (8.7 percent).

The districts differed from each other in several ways. Three districts offered dual-language programs, which were allowed in Massachusetts; however, the enrollment of ELLs in those programs was low: 3 percent in Boston, 2.1 percent in Brockton, and .1 percent in Holyoke. In one district, Weymouth, 7.4 percent of ELL parents had opted out of ELL services for their children altogether. Most districts had a low ratio of teachers qualified to teach ESL; in two districts, Wachusett and Worcester, the only instructional help ELLs received was from bilingual paraprofessionals—unlicensed teacher aides. The first language of most ELLs in the Brockton district was Cape Verdean; in Weymouth, Portuguese; and in Quincy, Mandarin. Spanish prevailed as the first language of the ELLs in the other seven districts.

The former ELLs did amazingly well compared to their peers who had never been designated "limited English." On the MCAS English language arts section, the former ELLs outperformed the never ELLs in five of the ten school districts. On the MCAS mathematics section, the former ELLs scored higher in seven of the districts. On the MCAS science section, the former ELLs scored higher in two of the schools (see figure 9.1).

The average ELL reached proficiency in 2.7 years. Twelve percent of the ELLs had not achieved English proficiency by the end of the study, with a majority of them having demonstrated a high level of need for special education services. Thus 88 percent of students who began as ELLs in kindergarten achieved English proficiency by the time the study concluded. In 2013–2014, the dropout average for ELLs in the study was 6.5 percent, whereas the overall dropout average for Massachusetts students was 2 percent.

Despite the increased enrollment and lack of services, ELLs in Wachusett came within 13 percentage points of meeting the district average in English language arts and within 4 percentage points of meeting the district average

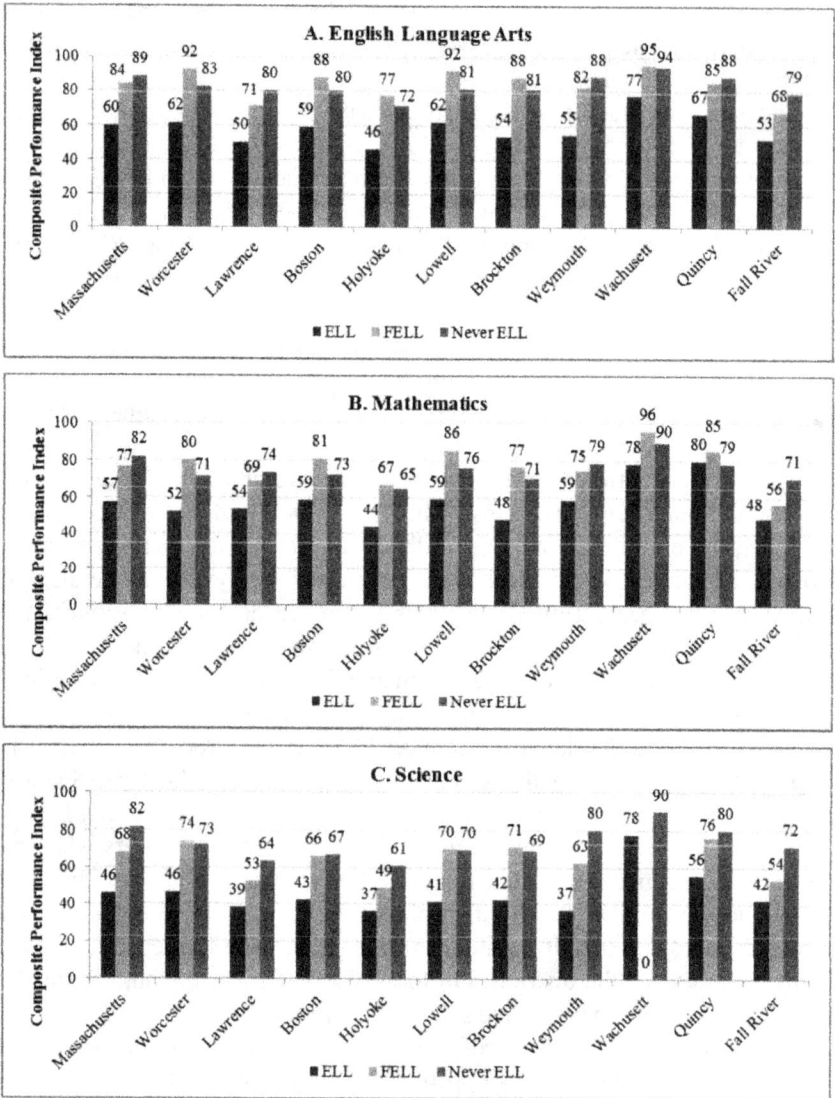

Figure 9.1. MCAS Composite Performance Index for ELLs, Former ELLs, and Students Who Were Never ELLs in English Language Arts, Mathematics, and Science

Source: American Institute for Research

in mathematics. ELLs in Quincy came within 2 percentage points of the average in mathematics.

Although many problems arose due to the continual increase of the ELL population in Massachusetts and the inability to service the needs of ELLs adequately, these schools did an excellent job in educating these children when compared to other states. Between the 2007–2008 and 2014–2015 school years, 34 percent of ELLs in federal Title III programs and 31 percent of all English learners on average in Massachusetts had become proficient in English and qualified to enter the mainstream annually. [52] Even dropouts identified as ELLs or former ELLs were likely to have reached a reasonable level of proficiency in English after attending Massachusetts schools for two or three years.

COMMON CORE STANDARDS

In July 2010 the Massachusetts Board of Elementary and Secondary Education (BESE) replaced the state's nationally recognized English and mathematics standards with Common Core English and mathematics standards. This guaranteed Massachusetts $250,000,000 in Race to the Top funds. In addition, in 2015 the state replaced its first-class science standards with the Next Generation Science Standards (NGSS), aligned to Common Core standards. [53]

Standra Stotsky opposed both of these changes, backing the End Common Core ballot question to let the state's citizens decide if they wanted to replace their first-rate standards with inferior ones. State Representative Alice Peisch, chairwoman of the education committee in the State House, said, "If that ballot question were to pass, that is six years of work that will be irrelevant." [54] The question never made it to the 2016 election ballot because Justice Margot Botsford of the state's Supreme Judicial Court decided that the section of the question asking for release of used test items was not related to the transparency of the state tests and made the entire question "incoherent."

BESE voted in 2016 to accept the recommendation of their education commissioner for a student assessment program called MCAS 2.0 as a compromise between expanding the use of PARCC tests and the legal requirement in the 1993 Massachusetts Education Reform Act (MERA) for a state-specific test in grade 10. This action led to a Common Core–based test called Next Generation MCAS, despite the fact the test bore no resemblance to the original MCAS and was not based on the state's pre–Common Core standards.

On October 18, 2017, Massachusetts education officials publicly released the results of the Next Generation MCAS in math and English, administered for the first time in the spring of 2017. The Associated Press reported that only half of Massachusetts students in grades 3–8 met or exceeded expectations. There was no information about who set the cutoffs at each tested grade level for each subject.

THE RETURN OF BILINGUAL EDUCATION

The 2002 Massachusetts education law requirements, based on Question 2, allowed children over the age of nine to receive waivers to participate in bilingual education, but this option was not pursued by the parents of ELLs. Dual-language programs were also lawful in Massachusetts districts, but the participation rate has been minimal, according to the AIR study. It appears that the parents of ELLs preferred the mandated SEI to any form of bilingual education.

Nevertheless, ignoring the will of the people and, most regrettably, the parents of ELLs, the Massachusetts Senate and House overwhelmingly acquiesced to the Massachusetts Association for Bilingual Education and voted in the summer of 2017 to eliminate the requirements of Question 2. Their two bills were reconciled and then signed into law by Governor Charlie Baker on November 22, 2017. Under the new law, districts are allowed to retain SEI or replace it with one or more bilingual programs at individual schools. Programs must be research-based best practice, contain subject matter content, and include an English language component.

To sell their programs, the pro-bilingual educators will have to develop a strong marketing plan to convince the parents of ELLs to sign up; even parents with little schooling have a hard time accepting the notion that their children will learn English well through instruction in Spanish. Moreover, most of these parents have noticed children in their communities succeeding in learning English quickly due to the near-elimination of bilingual education for the past fifteen years.

THE END OF THE MASSACHUSETTS MIRACLE?

State legislators and state board members in Massachusetts appear determined to change education in ways that reduce Massachusetts's educational strengths. They have harmed a school system considered the best in the country by replacing first-class standards in all subjects with Common Core's inferior standards and by allowing school districts to reimpose ineffectual bilingual education programs on the students of Massachusetts. Hopefully, in time, legislators more knowledgeable about education research, standards, tests, and the school curriculum will take office and repair the damage.

Acronym Guide

ACCESS	Assessing Comprehension and Communication in English State-to-State
ADE	Arizona Department of Education
AIMS	Arizona Instrument to Measure Standards
AIR	American Institutes for Research
AZELLA	Arizona English Language Learner Assessment
BESE	Board of Elementary and Secondary Education (MA)
CMAS	Colorado Measures of Academic Success
DESE	Department of Elementary and Secondary Education (MA)
DOE	US Department of Education
DPS	Denver Public Schools
EEOA	Equal Educational Opportunities Act
ELD	English language development
ELL	English language learner
ESEA	Elementary and Secondary Education Act
ESL	English as a second language
FEP	fluent English proficient
HB	House Bill
LAS	Language Assessment Scales
LEP	limited English proficient

MCAS	Massachusetts Comprehensive Assessment System
MCCCD	Maricopa County Community College District
MFLEP	monitored former limited English proficient
NAEP	National Assessment of Educational Progress
NCES	National Center for Educational Statistics
NCLB	No Child Left Behind
OCR	Office for Civil Rights
OELAS	Office of English Language Acquisition Services (AZ)
READ	Research in English Acquisition and Development
SAT-9	Stanford 9 Achievement Test
SEI	structured English immersion or sheltered English immersion
TBE	transitional bilingual education
TUSD	Tucson Unified School District

Notes

INTRODUCTION

1. Herman Badillo, *One Nation, One Standard* (New York: Sentinel of the Penguin Group, 2005), 62.

2. Ibid., 60–61.

3. James Crawford, *Bilingual Education: History, Politics, Theory and Practice* (Los Angeles: Bilingual Educational Services, 1999), 36.

4. Rosalie Pedalino Porter, *Forked Tongue* (New Brunswick, NJ: Transaction, 1995), 72–73, citing Silvia Rothfard, Maria Ariza, and Rafael Urrutia, *Evaluation of the Bilingual Curriculum Project: Final Report of a Three-Year Study* (Miami: Dade County Public Schools, 1987), ii.

5. Badillo, *One Nation, One Standard,* 60.

6. Ibid., 63.

7. Don Soifer, "Will Arizona Be Next? The Grand Canyon State Considers Reforming Bilingual Education," *Lexington Institute Issue Brief,* November 30, 1998, http://www.lexingtoninstitute.org/will-arizona-be-next-the-grand-canyon-state-considers-reforming-bilingual-education-?a=1&c=1136.

8. Crawford, *Bilingual Education,* 44–47.

9. Ibid., 53.

10. Linda Chavez, *Out of the Barrio* (New York: Basic Books, 1991), 19.

11. Crawford, *Bilingual Education,* 49–50.

12. General Court of the Commonwealth of Massachusetts, Chapter 71A, Section 4, from 1971–2003.

13. Alfredo Castaneda, PhD, P. Leslie Herold, PhD, and Manuel Ramirez III, PhD, "A New Philosophy of Education," *New Approaches to Bilingual, Bicultural Education* (1978): 3.

14. Ibid., 8.

15. Jim Cummins, "The Minority Language Child," *Bilingual and Multicultural Education: Canadian Perspectives,* chapter 5, ed. Stan Shapson and Vincent D'Oyley (Multilingual Matters 15, 1984), 85.

16. Charles L. Glenn, "Avoiding American's Mistakes," speech to a conference on educational equity in Stockholm, May 2001, 5. *European Journal for Education and Law Policy,* issue 1–2, chapter 5, Kluwer Academic Publishers, The Neverlands, 2003. (No longer available)

17. Wayne P. Thomas and Virginia Collier, "School Effectiveness for Language Minority Students." Paper disseminated by the National Clearinghouse for Bilingual Education (George

Mason University, 1997), 48. http://www.thomasandcollier.com/assets/1997_thomas-collier97-1.pdf.

18. Christine Rossell, "Mystery on the Bilingual Express: A Critique of the Thomas and Collier Study," *READ Perspectives* 5, no. 2 (fall 1998): 5–32.

19. Ibid., 12.

20. Charles Glenn, "Improving Schooling for Language Minority Children: A Research Agenda," A Review of the National Research Council Study, *READ Abstracts, Research and Policy Review* (May 1997): 1–2.

21. Mark Hugo Lopez and Marie T. Mora, "The Labor Market Effects of Bilingual Education Among Hispanic Workers," *READ Perspectives*, 5, no. 2 (fall 1998): 2.

22. Joseph M. Guzman, "Learning English," *Education Next* (fall 2002): 58–65.

1. RUNNING THE CALIFORNIA POLITICAL GAUNTLET

1. Amy Pule, "Pressure Grows to Reform Bilingual Education in State," *Los Angeles Times*, May 22, 1995, http://www.onenation.org/1995/052295.html.

2. Linda Chavez, *Out of the Barrio* (New York: Basic Books, 1991).

3. Rosalie Pedalino Porter, *Forked Tongue* (New Brunswick, NJ: Transaction, 1995).

4. Christine Rossell and Keith Baker, *Bilingual Education in Massachusetts: The Emperor Has No Clothes* (Boston: Pioneer Institute for Public Policy Research, 1996).

5. Pule, "Pressure Grows to Reform Bilingual Education."

6. Betsy Streisand, "Is It Hasta la Vista for Bilingual Ed?" *US News & World Report*, November 24, 1997, 36–38, http://www.onenation.org/article/is-it-hasta-la-vista-for-bilingual-ed/.

7. Gregory Rodriguez, "Speaking in Tongues: Divining Why California Latinos Voted as They Did on Proposition 227," *New Democrat*, July/August 1998, http://onenation.org/0798/0798.html.

8. Jay Mathews, *The Best Teacher in America* (New York: [An Owl Book] Paperback, Henry Holt & Company, August 1, 1989).

9. English for the Children website, http://www.onenation.org/.

10. "English Language in Public Schools, Proposition 227—Full Text of the Proposed Law," Voter Guide, 1998, http://www.onenation.org/fulltext.html.

11. Ibid.

12. Gregory Rodriguez, "Cause without Rebels," *LA Weekly*, August 15, 1997, http://www.onenation.org/1997/081597b.html.

13. Ron Unz, "English Isn't Racism" (letter), *La Opinion*, May 27, 1997, http://www.onenation.org/unzletter.html.

14. K. L. Billingsley, "Bilingual Education Targeted for Ballot," *Washington Times*, June 16, 1997, http://www.onenation.org/1997/061697.html.

15. Nick Anderson, "Times Orange County Poll: Public Schools Deserve Good Grades, Most Say," *Lost Angeles Times*, June 1, 1997, http://www.onenation.org/lat060197.html.

16. Robert B. Gunnison and Nanette Asimov, "Big Majorities in Poll Support Bilingual Limit: Shorter Transitions Advocated for Pupils Learning English," *San Francisco Chronicle*, December 9, 1997, http://www.onenation.org/1997/120997.html.

17. Ibid.

18. Ibid.

19. Ron Unz, "Field Poll Results," English for the Children, http://www.ronunz.org/1997/12/13/field-poll-results/.

20. Ron Unz, "A New Year's Resolution for California," English for the Children, http://onenation.org/0198/010198.html.

21. Phil Garcia, "Proposal Would Undercut Bilingual-Ed Foes," *Sacramento Bee*, January 8, 1998, http://onenation.org/0198/010898a.html.

22. Andrea Lampros, "Rush to Beat Vote on 227 May Be Too Little, Too Late," *Contra Costa Times*, April 22, 1998, http://onenation.org/0498/042298e.html.

23. "California Governor Pete Wilson Veto Message for SB 6," May 18, 1998, Language Policy Web Site & Emporium, http://www.languagepolicy.net/archives/wilson.htm.

24. June Kronholz, "Californians to Vote in June on Ending Bilingual Education," *Wall Street Journal*, January 9, 1998, http://onenation.org/0198/010998b.html.

25. William Wong, "Bilingual Education: The Next Cultural War," *San Francisco Examiner*, January 30, 1998, http://onenation.org/0198/013098c.html.

26. Tanya Schevitz, "Students Hold March in Concord: Protestors Target Lack of Educational Access," *San Francisco Chronicle*, April 23, 1998, http://onenation.org/0498/042398b.html.

27. Tina Nguyen, "Harvard Panel Assails Bilingual Measure," *Los Angeles Times*, April 26, 1998, http://onenation.org/0498/042698a.html.

28. Pam King, "Bilingual Education Foes Make Their Cases," *Contra Costa Times*, April 30, 1998, http://onenation.org/0498/043098e.html.

29. John M. Broder, "Clinton Criticizes California Effort to Cut Bilingual Education," *New York Times*, May 3, 1998, http://www.nytimes.com/1998/05/03/us/clinton-criticizes-california-effort-to-cut-bilingual-education.html.

30. Louis Freedberg, "Education Secretary Blasts Proposition 227," *San Francisco Chronicle*, April 28, 1998, http://onenation.org/0498/042898e.html.

31. Jim Newton, "Riordan Plans Ads in Spanish Backing Measure," *Los Angeles Times*, May 21, 1998, http://onenation.org/0598/052198e.html.

32. Phil Garcia, "Spanish-TV Mogul Funds Prop 227 Foes," *Sacramento Bee*, May 22, 1998, http://www.onenation.org/article/spanish-tv-mogul-funds-prop-227-foes/.

33. "Review of Prop 227 Campaign Spending," English for the Children, http://www.onenation.org/finan.html.

34. Garcia, "Spanish-TV mogul funds Prop 227 Foes."

35. Sherri Annis, "Despite Massive Opposition Campaign, Proposition 227 Sweeps to Landslide Victory," English for the Children, http://www.onenation.org/pr060598.html.

36. "Review of Prop. 227 Campaign Spending."

37. Ibid.

2. UNDER ATTACK

1. Sheri Annis, "Clinton Administration Legal Analysts Conclude Prop 227 Is Fully Constitutional," English for the Children, May 4, 1998, http://www.onenation.org/pr050498.html.

2. Ibid.

3. Charles Legge, District Judge, "Order Denying Motion for Preliminary Injunction," *Valeria G. et al. v. Pete Wilson et al.*, July 15, 1998, http://cmmr.usc.edu/227/LeggeDecision227.PDF.

4. "State Teachers Association Loses Challenge to Portion of Proposition 227," *Sacramento Bee*, September 15, 1999, http://www.onenation.org/article/state-teachers-association-loses-challenge-to-portion-of-proposition-227/.

5. "San Jose Schools Ruled Exempt from Prop 227," *Contra Costa Times*, December 18, 1998, http://www.languagepolicy.net/archives/CCT21.htm.

6. Ibid.

7. Ibid.

8. "Opinion of Bill Lockyer, Attorney General, Anthony S. Da Vigo, Deputy Attorney General," Office of the Attorney General, State of California, February 25, 2000, ag.ca.gov/opinions/pdfs/99-802.pdf.

9. James Crawford, "English-Only vs. English-Only: A Tale of Two Initiatives: California and Arizona," 2000, http://www.languagepolicy.net/archives/203-227.htm.

10. Johanna Haver, "Time to End Bilingual Education," *Arizona Republic*, June 12, 2000, http://www.onenation.org/0006/061200.html.

11. Sheri Annis, "English for the Children Enforcement Project: Oceanside Unified Denounced by CA Department of Education for Doubling Immigrant Test Scores, Defended by

Prop. 227 Author Ron Unz," English for the Children (press release), October 3, 2000, http://www.onenation.org/0010/pr100300.html.

12. Sherry Parmet, "Oceanside Defends English Immersion," *San Diego Union-Tribune*, October 24, 2000, http://www.onenation.org/0010/102400b.html.

13. Samuel Casey Carter, *No Excuses: Seven Principals of Low-Income Schools Who Set the Standard for High Achievement* (Washington, DC: Heritage Foundation, 1999), 23–26.

14. Ken Noonan and Mark Wyland, "Bringing English to State's Schools," *San Diego Union- Tribune*, May 9, 2002.

15. Christine H. Rossell, "The Near End of Bilingual Education," *Education Next* (fall 2003): 49.

16. This time frame was based on classroom research conducted by Rossell over decades of visiting ESL classrooms and talking to ELLs who were playing at computers because they no longer needed the intensive ESL that other students in the class were receiving. Almost all of these students had been in the United States for at least two years and stated that they could understand almost everything their teachers were teaching them by the middle of their first year—that is, at the Christmas break.

17. Rossell, "The Near End of Bilingual Education," 48.

18. Ibid., 49.

19. Laurie Olsen, *Reparable Harm: Fulfilling the Unkept Promise of Educational Opportunity for California's Long-Term English Learners* (Long Beach, CA: Californians Together Research and Policy Publication, 2010), 15, available at http://www.laurieolsen.com/uploads/2/5/4/9/25499564/reparableharm2ndedition.pdf.

20. "Table 204.20. Number and percentage of public school students participating in programs for English language learners, by state: Selected years, 2002–2003 to 2012–2013," Digest of Education Statistics, National Center for Education Statistics.

21. "Facts about English Learners in California—CalEdFacts," California Department of Education, https://www.cde.ca.gov/ds/sd/cb/cefelfacts.asp.

22. Ibid. "Facts about English Learners in California."

23. Joanne Jacobs, "Learning English," EducationNext, Winter 2016/vol. 16, No. 1, http://educationnext.org/learning-english-accountability-common-core-college-instruction/.

24. "California: Title III Program—English Learners," *ED Data Express: Data about Elementary and Secondary Schools in the U.S.*, US Department of Education, ED.gov, https://eddataexpress.ed.gov/state-tables-main.cfm.

25. Ibid. These computations were made by averaging the fourth grade, eighth grade, and high school percentage rates of all students in California during the specified years and comparing that number with the state's corresponding yearly MFLEP percentages. All data was found at the Ed Data Express website.

26. National Center for Education Statistics, "Common Core of Data: America's Public Schools," Table 1: Public high school 4-year adjusted cohort graduation rate (ACGR), 2014–2015. US Department of Education, ED.gov, https://eddataexpress.ed.gov/state-tables-main.cfm.

3. LATINOS VS. LATINOS

1. "Maria Escalante Mendoza, Statewide Chair, English for the Children of Arizona Campaign," English for the Children, http://www.onenation.org/azcampaign.html#M.

2. Maria Mendoza, telephone interview with the author, October 12, 2000.

3. Ibid.

4. Hector Ayala, interview with author, September 2003.

5. Ibid.

6. Mendoza, telephone interview.

7. Ibid.

8. Margaret Garcia Dugan, interview with the author, November 25, 2000.

9. Jeff Alvarez, telephone interview with the author, September 13, 2003.

10. Dugan, interview.

11. Maria Mendoza and Hector Ayala, "English Language Education for Children in Public Schools, AZ Prop 203," January 6, 1999, English for the Children, http://www.onenation.org/aztext.html; italics mine.

12. Ibid.

13. Ibid.

14. James Crawford, "English-Only vs. English-Only: A Tale of Two Initiatives: California and Arizona," 2000, http://www.languagepolicy.net/archives/203-227.htm.

15. Tony Paniaga, KVOA/Channel 4, Tucson, AZ, August 14, 1998, https://www.youtube.com/watch?v=LyOng2M2oTs.

16. Ibid.

17. Sarah Tully Tapia, "Rowdy Group Disrupts Anti-Bilingual Education Event," *Arizona Daily Star*, Jan. 7, 1999, http://www.onenation.org/article/rowdy-group-disrupts-anti-bilingual-education-event/.

18. Channel 12 News, KPNX/Channel 12, Phoenix, AZ, January 6, 1999.

19. Karina Bland, "Report Faults Bilingual Ed," *Arizona Republic*, February 2, 1999, http://www.onenation.org/9902/020299c.html.

20. Lisa Graham Keegan, "English Acquisition Services: A Summary of Bilingual Programs and English as a Second Language Programs for School Year 1997–8," *Report of the Superintendent of Public Instruction to the Arizona Legislature*, January 1999, cover letter.

21. Ibid., cover letter.

22. Ibid., 13–14.

23. Lori Baker, "Committee Looking at Improving Bilingual Ed," *Arizona Republic*, December 8, 1999, http://www.onenation.org/9912/120899a.html.

24. *Face the State*, KSAZ/Channel 10, Phoenix, AZ, February 7, 1999, https://www.youtube.com/watch?v=FMZ71ysnk14.

25. "What's New in Reclassification Research?" *The Southwest Comprehensive Center at the Center for the Education and Study of Diverse Populations* (New Mexico Highlands University, Rio Rancho, NM, May 2000), presented to the Arizona Revised Statutes 15-756 Task Force Members in June 2000.

26. Maria Leon, "Bill Threatens to Limit Bilingual Education," *El Independiente*, April 1998, accessed September 3, 2003, http://journalism.arizona.edu/searh/node/archives.

27. Don Soifer, "Will Arizona Be Next? The Grand Canyon State Considers Reforming Bilingual Education," *Lexington Institute* Issue Brief, November 30, 1998, http://www.lexingtoninstitute.org/will-arizona-be-next-the-grand-canyon-state-considers-reforming-bilingual-education-.

28. David Madrid, "Bilingual Education Bills in Duel," *Tucson Citizen*, March 26, 1999, http://www.onenation.org/9903/032699b.html.

29. Ibid.

30. Ruben Navarrette Jr., "Legislature's Lapse Leaves Bilingual Education to Voters," *Arizona Republic*, May 5, 1999, http://www.onenation.org/9905/050599.html.

31. Paul Davenport, "Compromise on Bilingual Education Focuses on Parents' Rights, Study," Associated Press, May 4, 1999, http://www.onenation.org/article/compromise-on-bilingual-education-focuses-on-parents-rights-study/

32. Ruben Navarrette Jr., "Sen. Lopez's Stance on Bilingual Education a Mystery," *Arizona Republic*, February 10, 1999.

33. Jorge Amselle, "Ingles, Si: Hispanic Parents Want What's Best for Their Children—and the Country," *National Review*, September 30, 1996.

34. Lori Baker, "Stanford Achievement Test Scores by School Distridt," *Arizona Republic*, July 2, 1998.

35. Ibid.

36. Ibid.

37. Chip Scutari, "Alhambra's Success Bucks Poverty Trend," *Arizona Republic*, September 21, 2001.

38. Michael Barone, "The National Interest: In Plain English," *US News & World Report*, May 29, 2000, 47.

39. Johanna Haver, "Time to End Bilingual Education," *Arizona Republic*, June 12, 2000, http://www.onenation.org/0006/061200.html.

40. Daniel Gonzalez, "Bilingual Schooling Targeted," *Arizona Republic*, June 28, 2000, A12.

41. Ibid.

42. Elisa Bongiovanni, "Petitions Filed for Initiative to Dismantle Bilingual Education," Associated Press, June 27, 2000, http://www.onenation.org/0006/062700.html.

43. Jacques Steinberg, "Increase in Test Scores Counters Dire Forecasts for Bilingual Ban," *New York Times*, August 20, 2000, http://www.onenation.org/0008/082000.html.

44. "California Scores," *Wall Street Journal*, August 23, 2000, http://www.onenation.org/0008/082300a.html.

45. "Bilingual Education Fails Test, Exposing Deeper Problem," *USA Today*, August 28, 2000, http://www.onenation.org/editorial/bilingual-education-fails-test-exposing-deeper-problem/.

46. Maria Mendoza, "Rep. Laura Knaperek Endorses Prop 203, Proposes 'English for the Families' Act," English for the Children of Arizona Project (press release), September 21, 2000, http://www.onenation.org/0009/pr092100.html.

47. Don Soifer, "Test Scores Show Failure of Bilingual Ed," *School Reform News*, 4, no. 10 (October 2000): 3.

48. Stephen Krashen, "Comments on Johanna Haver, *Structured English Immersion*," April 2003, http://www.sdkrashen.com/content/articles/response_to_haver.pdf.

49. Daniel Gonzales, "Tribes Protest Prop. 203," *Arizona Republic*, October 14, 2000, http://www.onenation.org/0010/101400.html.

50. Daniel Gonzales, "Indians Protest Push for English," *Arizona Republic*, October 13, 2000, http://www.onenation.org/0010/101300.html.

51. Attorney General Janet Napolitano, "To the Honorable Jack Jackson, Chairman of Citizens Clean Elections Commission re: Application of Proposition 203 to Schools Serving the Navajo Nation" 101-006 (R00-062), February 15, 2001, 1, https://www.azag.gov/sites/default/files/I01-006.pdf.

52. Richard Ruelas, "American Way to Save Bilingual Education," *Arizona Republic*, October 18, 2000, http://www.onenation.org/opinion/american-way-to-save-bilingual-ed/.

53. Arizona State University Law School Federalist Society-Sponsored Debate, October 26, 2000, videotape of entire debate provided to the author by ASU Professor Jeff MacSwan.

54. Daniel Gonzales, "Bilingual Education Gets Rebuke from State Voters," *Arizona Republic*, November 8, 2000.

55. Ibid.

4. CLOSING THE "LOOPHOLES"

1. Daniel Gonzáles, "Arizona Win Encourages Bilingual-Ed Opponents," *Arizona Republic*, November 20, 2000, http://www.onenation.org/0011/112000a.htm.

2. Daniel Gonzáles, "Bilingual-Ed Supporter: Defy Prop 203," *Arizona Republic*, November 9, 2000, http://www.onenation.org/article/bilingual-ed-supporter-defy-prop-203/.

3. Anne Ryman, "Keegan to Allow Bilingual Teaching," *Arizona Republic*, January 10, 2001, http://www.onenation.org/article/keegan-to-allow-bilingual-teaching/.

4. Ibid.

5. Ibid.

6. Hipolito R. Corella, "Keegan Says She'll Enforce Prop 203," *Arizona Daily Star*, January 11, 2001, http://www.onenation.org/0101/011101b.htm.

7. Ryman, "Keegan to Allow Bilingual Teaching."

8. Ron Unz, "Above the Law in Arizona?" *National Review*, January 12, 2001, http://www.onenation.org/0101/011201.htm.

9. Ryman, "Keegan to Allow Bilingual Teaching."

10. Corella, "Keegan Says She'll Enforce Prop 203."

11. Maria Mendoza and Hector Ayala, "English Language Education for Children in Public Schools," January 6, 1999, http://www.onenation.org/aztext.html.

12. Salvador Gabaldón, "Prop 203 Won't Banish Bilingual Ed" *Arizona Daily Star*, November 26, 2000, http://www.onenation.org/0011/112600a.htm.

13. Joe Eddie Lopez, "Bilingual Education Waivers," e-mail to the author et al., September 4, 2001.

14. Mendoza and Ayala, "English Language Education for Children in Public Schools."

15. Ibid.

16. Mary Bustamante and Dina Doolen, "Bilingual Ed: Fight Goes On," *Arizona Citizen*, July 9, 2001, http://www.onenation.org/0107/070901.htm.

17. Sara Thorson, "A Year Later: Schools Grapple with English Immersion Law," *State Press*, April 2, 2002, http://www.onenation.org/article/a-year-later/ .

18. "A Visit with Jaime Molera: An Inside Look at the Man and His Mission," *AEA Advocate* (October/November 2001): 15.

19. Mendoza and Ayala, "English Language Education for Children in Public Schools."

20. Arthur H. Rotstein, "Tucson Educators Tell Lawmakers of Steps Planned to Comply with Prop 203," Associated Press, July 24, 2001, http://www.onenation.org/0107/072401.htm.

21. Ibid.

22. Robert Robb, "Activist Judge, Vague Laws Trump Our Elected Officials," *Arizona Republic*, September 9, 2001, accessed October 7, 2010. Can be accessed through www.newsbank.com.

23. READ Institute, "Phase IV—Chapter 1: Nogales Unified School District, Programs for English Language Learner Students, Arizona Department of Education English Acquisition Program Cost Study—Phase I-IV, May 2001, IV, 37 (Section IV, p 37).

24. Committee on Education and the Workforce, House of Representatives, One Hundred Sixth Congress, First Session, "Examining the Bilingual Education Act," hearing held in Washington, DC (June 24, 1999), http://commdocs.house.gov/committees/edu/hedcew6-50.000/hedcew6-50.htm.

25. Chip Scutari, "Former Lawmaker Seeks Schools Post," *Arizona Republic*, March 19, 2002.

26. Ibid.

27. Ibid.

28. "Horne Criticizes Molera for Playing Race Card," Media Advisory, Tom Horne for Superintendent of Public Instruction, For Immediate Release Wednesday, March 20, 2002. Contact Art Harding [campaign director].

29. Maria Mendoza, "English for the Children of Arizona Leaders Endorse Tom Horne, Oppose Jaime Molera in Race for State Superintendent of Schools" (press release), English for the Children of Arizona, July 16, 2002.

30. Mel Meléndez, "Molera Backs District on its Spanish Ban," *Arizona Republic*, August 20, 2002, http://azbilingualed.org/AABE%20Site/Bilingual%20Education%20in%20the%20News_files/molera_backs_district_on_its_spa.htm.

31. "Primary Results Offer Unpleasant Surprises; Our Stand: Good Folks Ushered Out," *Arizona Republic*, September 11, 2002, accessed December 27, 2010. Can be accessed at https://azcentral.newspapers.com.

32. Joseph Guzman, "Learning English," *Education Next* (fall 2002): 64–65.

33. "Superintendent Tom Horne Announces New Guidelines for Implementing English Immersion Instruction for Arizona Children" (press release), Arizona Department of Education, December 17, 2002.

34. Ibid.

35. Jennifer Sterba, Jonathan Higuera, and Barrett Marson, "Bilingual Waivers Restricted," *Arizona Daily Star*, February 14, 2003.

36. Mary Ann Zehr, "New Arizona Chief Clamps Down on Bilingual Rules, *Education Week*, Vol. 22, Issue 24, 14, February 26, 2003.

37. Ibid.

38. Ibid.

39. Ignacio Ibarra, "English—Only OK for Border Students," *Arizona Daily Star*, April 9, 2003.

40. Ibid.

41. Ibid.

42. Ibid.

5. FROM POLITICAL IMPASSE TO THE US SUPREME COURT

1. *Lau v. Nichols*, 414 US 563 (1974).

2. Arizona Senate Research Staff, "Flores v. Arizona," *Arizona State Senate Issue Paper*, Phoenix Arizona, August 27, 2008, 1, https://www.azleg.gov/briefs/Senate/FLORES%20V%20ARIZONA.pdf.

3. Chip Scutari, "What Price English? Budget Crisis Complicates Bilingual Funding Fight," *Arizona Republic*, November 15, 2001, http://www.onenation.org/0111/111501.htm.

4. Ibid.

5. Sjoberg Evasheck Consulting, LLC, "Executive Summary," *Arizona Department of Education English Acquisition Program Cost Study—Phases I through IV*, May 2001, 2.

6. Ibid.

7. Rosalie Pedalino Porter and Scott K. Baker, "Phase IV, Chapter 1, Nogales Unified School District: Programs for English Language Learner Students, K–12," *Arizona Department of Education English Acquisition Program Cost Study—Phases I through IV*, May 2001, Phase IV—Chapter 1, 37.

8. Chip Scutari, "English at What Cost?" *Arizona Republic*, May 23, 2001, http://www.onenation.org/0105/052301a.htm.

9. Sarah Auerback, "New Law May Break Long Deadlock in Arizona's ELL Court Case," *ELL Outlook*, March 3, 2006, http://www.coursecrafters.com/ELL-Outlook/2006/mar_apr/ELLOutlookITIArticle4.htm.

10. Ibid.

11. Eric J. Bistrow, *Collected Works of Eric J. Bistrow*, Self-published (Phoenix, Arizona: printed by Alphagraphics and bound by Roswell Bookbinding), December 2017, 346.

12. Ibid.

13. Ibid.

14. Ibid., 347.

15. Susan Carroll, "Judge Seeks End to Education Impasse by Jailing Governor and GOP leaders," *Arizona Republic*, November 1, 2005,http://www.azcentral.com/families/education/articles/1101flores01.html.

16. Ibid.

17. Ibid.

18. Bistrow, *Collected Works of Eric Bistrow*, 347.

19. Kathy Scott, "Judge's Ruling Insults ELL Students in Nogales," *Nogales International*, January 26, 2006. Can be accessed at https://www.nogalesinternational.com/.

20. Ibid.

21. Bistrow, *Collected Works of Eric Bistrow*, 348.

22. Ibid.

23. Janet Napolitano, "State Must Find Way to Help Our Kids Learn English," *Arizona Republic*, March 5, 2006, http://www.azbilingualed.org/News_2006/state_must_find_way_to_help_our_kids_learn_Eng.htm.

24. Bistrow, *Collected Works of Eric Bistrow*, 349.

25. Ibid.

26. Arizona Senate Research Staff, "Flores vs. Arizona," *Arizona State Senate Issue Paper*, August 27, 2008, 3–4.

27. "Transcript of Evidentiary Hearing, Day One, Before the Honorable Raner C. Collins," United States District Judge, *Miriam Flores, et al., Plaintiffs, vs. State of Arizona, et al.,*

Defendants, United States District Court, District of Arizona (Docket No. CV92-596 TUC-RCC, Tucson, AZ) January 9, 2007, 19.

28. Ibid., 30.
29. Ibid., 31–32.
30. Ibid., 33–79.
31. Ibid., 85–86.
32. Ibid., 95.
33. Ibid., 101.
34. Ibid., 115.
35. Ibid., 96–97.
36. Ibid., 113.
37. Ibid., 130.
38. Bistrow, *Collected Works of Eric Bistrow*, 350.
39. Arizona Senate Research Staff, "Flores v. Arizona," *Arizona State Senate Issue Paper*, Phoenix Arizona, August 27, 2008, 4, https://www.azleg.gov/briefs/Senate/FLORES%20V%20ARIZONA.pdf.
40. Robert Robb, "A Legal Leap into Neverland: Latest English-Learner Ruling Defies Logic, Translation," *Arizona Republic*, March 28, 2007.
41. Ibid.
42. "Supreme Court to Hear Arizona ELL Case," *Education Week*, Vol. 28, Issue 18, 20–21, January 9, 2009.
43. Bistrow, *Collected Works of Eric Bistrow*, 353.
44. Ibid.
45. "Official—Subject to Final Review," Alderson Reporting Company, Washington, D.C, https://www.supremecourt.gov/oral_arguments/argument_transcripts/2008/08-289.pdf.
46. Ibid., 5–13.
47. Ibid., 14.
48. Ibid., 20–22.
49. Ibid., 22–23.
50. Ibid., 26.
51. Ibid., 26–28.
52. Ibid., 32–36.
53. Ibid., 36–37.
54. Ibid., 37–39.
55. Ibid., 39.
56. Ibid., 40.
57. Ibid., 40–42.
58. Ibid., 49–60.
59. Miriam Flores et al., "On Writs of Certiorari to the United States Court of Apeals for the Ninth Circuit" (June 25, 2009), 14, https://www.supremecourt.gov/opinions/08pdf/08-289.pdf.
60. Ibid., 23–30.
61. Ibid., 22.
62. Ibid., 34.
63. J. Bryers, "Dissenting the Supreme Court of the U.S." in *The Court's Dissenting Opinion*, 3.
64. Ibid., 42.
65. Pat Kossan, "Court Eases Rules on English Learner Program," *Arizona Republic*, June 25, 2009.
66. Ibid.
67. Bistrow, *Collected Work of Eric Bistrow*, 354.
68. Ibid.

6. IMPLEMENTING STRUCTURED ENGLISH IMMERSION

1. House Bill 2064, Arizona House of Representatives, 47th Legislature, 2nd Regular Session, 2006, 7–8.

2. Ibid.

3. Minutes of the Meeting of the Arizona ELL Task Force, September 21, 2006.

4. Ibid.

5. Minutes of the Meeting of the Arizona ELL Task Force, November 20, 2006.

6. Minutes of the Meeting of the Arizona ELL Task Force, November 30, 2006.

7. "Structured English Immersion Models of the Arizona English Language Learners Task Force," Office of English Language Acquisition Services, Arizona Department of Education, revised December 2014, 1–9, https://cms.azed.gov/home/GetDocumentFile?id=55257a8f1130c008a0c55ce3.

8. More detailed information about the training can be found at http://www.azed.gov/oelas/sei-endorsement.

9. "New course for English learners off to good start," *Arizona Daily Star*, August 29, 2008, https://tucson.com/news/new-course-for-english-learners-off-to-good-start/article_a1df9b90-6c5b-5303-9eba-c46aede3c760.html.

10. Debra K. Davenport, Auditor General, "Arizona English Language learner Program Fiscal Year 2010," Report No. 11-06, June 2011, 16, https://www.azauditor.gov/sites/default/files/ELL_Report.pdf.

11. Alan E. Maguire, Arizona ELL Task Force chairman (2006–2012), affirmed the information in an email to the author, June 21, 2018.

12. Arizona Title III–English learners, English language proficiency, all English learners, Ed.gov Ed Data Express: Data about elementary and secondary schools in the U.S.A. Arizona Title III–English learners, Monitored former limited English proficient students, Ed.gov Ed Data Express: Data about elementary and secondary schools in the U.S.A, https://eddataexpress.ed.gov/state-tables/mail.cfm

13. Minutes of Arizona ELL Task Force Meetings, 2006 to 2012.

14. "EL-Demographics," Office of English Language Acquisition Services, Arizona Department of Education, http://www.azed.gov/oelas/el-demographics-2012-2013/ and http://www.azed.gov/oelas/el-demographics-2013-2014/.

15. "Arizona: Title III Program—English learners," *ED Data Express: Data about Elementary and Secondary Schools in the U.S.*, US Department of Education, ED.gov, https://eddataexpress.ed.gov/state-tables-main.cfm. Note: These computations were made by averaging the 4th, 8th, and high school percentage rates of all students in Arizona during the specified years and comparing that number with the state's corresponding yearly MFLEP percentages. All data was found at the Ed Data Express website.

16. "El Demographics 2016-2017," OELAS, Arizona Department of Education, http://www.azed.gov/oelas/el-demographics-2016-2017/.

17. "Best High Schools," U.S. News & World Report, 2018, https://www.usnews.com/education/best-high-schools/arizona/districts/nogales-unified-district/nogales-high-school-1024.

18. Nogales High School, Great Schools School Profile, https://www.greatschools.org/arizona/nogales/1975-Nogales-High-School/.

7. RESISTANCE TO CHANGE IN NEW YORK CITY

1. Daniel Weintraub, "Unz Anti-Bilingual Ed Crusade Goes Nationwide," *Sacramento Bee*, December 24, 2000, onenation.org/0012/122400a.htm.

2. Jacques Steinberg, "Answers to an English Question: Instead of Ending Program, New York May Offer a Choice," *New York Times*, October 22, 2000, http://www.onenation.org/0010/102200.html.

3. Randy M. Mastro, *Report of the Task Force on Bilingual Education to Mayor Rudolph Giuliani*, presented to the City of New York, December 15, 2000, 8–9.

4. Ibid., 7.

5. Ibid., 10.

6. Michael R. Blood and Paul H. B. Shin, "Mayor Rips Push to Up Funding for Bilingual Ed," *New York Daily News*, December 22, 2000, http://www.nydailynews.com/archives/news/mayor-rips-push-funding-bilingual-ed-article-1.892130.

7. Ron Unz, "Bilingual Education Lives On," *New York Times*, March 2, 2001, http://www.onenation.org/0103/030201.htm.

8. Lynette Holloway, "Bilingual Program Overhaul May Be Scaled Back, Levy Says," *New York Times*, July 31, 2001, https://www.nytimes.com/2001/07/31/nyregion/bilingual-program-overhaul-may-be-scaled-back-levy-says.html.

9. "Bothered, Bewildered by Bilingual Ed," *New York Daily News*, July 18, 2001, http://www.onenation.org/0107/071801c.htm.

10. John Tierney, "In Debate, Candidates Go against Type," *New York Times*, November 2, 2001, http://www.onenation.org/0111/110201.htm.

11. Office of English Language Learners, *Diverse Learners on the Road to Success: The Performance of New York City's English Language Learners* (New York: New York City Department of Education, 2009), 6.

12. Division of English Language Learners and Student Support, *English Language Learners Demographics Report for the 2015–16 School Year* (New York: New York City Department of Education, 2016), 39.

13. "Chancellor Fariña Announces 38 New Bilingual Programs," NYC Department of Education, April 4, 2016, http://schools.nyc.gov/Offices/mediarelations/NewsandSpeeches/2015-2016/Chancellor+Farina+Announces+38+New+Bilingual+Programs.htm.

14. Joanne Jacobs, "Learning English," *EducationNext* (winter 2016), http://www.educationnext.org/learning-english-accountability-common-core-college-instruction.

15. "Chancellor Fariña Announces 38 New Bilingual Programs."

16. Ibid.

17. "Chancellor Fariña Announces Citywide Bilingual Expansion, Bringing 68 New Programs to Schools this Fall," New York City Department of Education, February 28, 2017, http://schools.nyc.gov/Offices/mediarelations/NewsandSpeeches/2016-2017/BilingualExpansion.htm.

18. Rosalie P. Porter, e-mail to the author, October 14, 2017.

19. "New York: Title III program—English Learners," *ED Data Express: Data about Elementary and Secondary Schools in the U.S.*," US Department of Education, ED.gov, https://eddataexpress.ed.gov/state-tables-main.cfm. The state test data from one state cannot be compared to that of another state because each state creates its own tests. These computations were made by averaging the 4th, 8th, and high school percentage rates of all students in New York during the specified years and comparing that number with the state's corresponding yearly MFLEP percentages. All data was provided by the Ed Data Express.

20. Marcus A. Winters, "Why the Gap? English Language Learners and New York City Charter schools," *Manhattan Institute Civic Report* 93 (October 2014), 8–9.

21. Winters, 1.

8. COLORADO'S MISSED OPPORTUNITY

1. Cathy Cummins, "Pollster: Colorado Backs Curbs on Bilingual Teaching," *Rocky Mountain News*, June 4, 1998, http://www.onenation.org/0698/060498af.html.

2. "Warning from California: Could Colorado Follow California's Lead and Banish Bilingual Education? Yes, If Federal Officials Don't Reconsider Their Intransigence," *Rocky Mountain News*, June 6, 1998, http://www.onenation.org/0698/060698f.html.

3. Ibid.

4. Tustin Amole, "DPS Receives Federal Warning: School District Failing to Adequately Instruct Non-English Speaking Students, Report Says," *Rocky Mountain News*, August 1, 1997, http://www.onenation.org/1997/080197.html.

5. Carlos Illescas, "DPS Bilingual Plan a Cause for Concern," *Denver Post*, Februray 28, 1999, http://www.onenation.org/9902/022899c.html.

6. Ibid.

7. Ibid.

8. Julie Jargon, "Language Barrier," *Denver Westword*, August 10, 2000, http://www.onenation.org/0008/081000a.html.

9. Eric Hubler, "Denver Schools Chief Forced Out," *Denver Post*, May 17, 2000, http://extras.denverpost.com/news/news0517a.htm.

10. Jargon, "Language Barrier."

11. Ibid.

12. Valerie Richardson, "Colorado Teacher Leads Push for English-Immersion Plan," *Washington Times*, June 19, 2000, http://www.onenation.org/0006/061900.html.

13. Fred Brown, "Bilingual Ed Issue Won't Be on Ballot," *Denver Post*, July 11, 2000, http://www.onenation.org/0007/071100.html.

14. Ibid.

15. Eric Hubler, "Bilingual Fray May Go to Ballot," *Denver Post*, June 20, 2001, http://www.onenation.org/0106/062001a.htm.

16. Rita Montero, "Former Denver School Board Members Endorse Ballot Initiative Campaign to Dismantle Bilingual Education in Colorado" (press release), English for the Children, November 30, 2001, http://www.onenation.org/0111/113001a.htm.

17. Ibid.

18. John Sanko, "Bilingual-Education Flap a Step Closer to Ballot," *Rocky Mountain News*, December 6, 2001, http://www.onenation.org/0112/120601.htm.

19. Kathy Escamilla, Sheila Shannon, Silvana Carlos, and Jorge Garcia "Breaking the Code: Colorado's Defeat of the Anti-Bilingual Education Initiative (Amendment 31)," *Bilingual Research Journal* 27, no. 3, (Fall 2003): 361, https://nepc.colorado.edu/publication/breaking-code-colorados-defeat-anti-bilingual-education-initiative-amendment-31.

20. "Background," Colorado English Language Education, Initiative 31 (2002), *Ballotpedia* (website) https://ballotpedia.org/Colorado_English_Language_Education,_Initiative_31_(2002).

21. Ibid.

22. "Bilingual Balderdash," *Wall Street Journal*, October 11, 2002, http://online.wsj.com/article/0,SB103430393280794076.djm,00.html.

23. Ibid.

24. Ibid.

25. Escamilla, Shannon, Carlos, and Garcia, *Breaking the Code*, 374–75.

26. "Total Number of English Learners (ELs) in Grades K–12," Culturally and Linguistically Diverse Learners in Colorado, State of the State 2016, Colorado Department of Education, http://www.cde.state.co.us/cde_english/elstateofthestate.

27. "ELA by the Numbers," *ELA Handbook for Schools*, Denver Public Schools, August 2016, http://thecommons.dpsk12.org/cms/lib/CO01900837/Centricity/domain/107/ela_department_page/principal%20resources/ELA-Handbook-for-Schools.pdf.

28. Department of English Language Acquisition, *The Denver Public Schools Allocation Guidelines* (Denver: Denver Public Schools, 2016), viii, 4, http://thecommons.dpsk12.org/cms/lib/CO01900837/Centricity/domain/107/ela_department_page/principal%20resources/Language_Allocation_Guidelines_ECE-5.pdf.

29. Chris Halsne and Chris Koeberl, "DPS Again Fails to Comply with Federal Mandate for English Language Learners," FOX31/Colorado's Own Channel 2, Denver, October 5, 2016.

30. Yesenia Robles, "Three Decades after Order, Denver Schools Still Struggle to Teach English," *Denver Post*, October 25, 2014, last updated April 26, 2016, https://www.denverpost.com/2014/10/25/three-decades-after-order-denver-schools-still-struggle-to-teach-english/.

31. Ibid.

32. Halsne and Koeberl, "DPS Again Fails to Comply."

33. Robles, "Three Decades after Order."

34. Paul. E. Martinez, "Independent Monitor Report: Congress of Hispanic educators et al., Petitioners, v. School District No. 1, Denver, Colorado" submitted to U.S. District Judge Richard Matsch and All Formal Parties to the Case, February 26, 2016, 9, https://www.clearinghouse.net/chDocs/public/ED-CO-0001-0023.pdf.

35. Susana Cordova, Acting Superintendent, Denver Public Schools, Letter to the Members of the Colorado State Board of Education, February 4, 2016, https://www.documentcloud.org/documents/2710402-DPS-Comments-on-Proposed-READ-Act-Rule-Change.html.

36. "Colorado: Title III program—English Learners," *ED Data Express: Data about Elementary and Secondary Schools in the U.S.* US Department of Education, ED.gov, https://eddataexpress.ed.gov/state-tables-main.cfm. The state test data from one state cannot be compared to that of another state because each state creates its own tests. These computations were made by averaging the 4th, 8th, and high school percentage rates of all students in Colorado during the specified years and comparing that number with the state's corresponding yearly MFLEP percentages. All data was provided by the Ed Data Express.

37. Data can be viewed online on 3rd page of report under "Third Grade Reading." https://www.denvergov.org/content/dam/denvergov/Portals/713/documents/2014_Data--Lisa/DPS%20Fact%20Sheet.pdf.

9. MASSACHUSETTS'S RISE AND FALL

1. Porter wrote about those experiences in her book *Forked Tongue: The Politics of Bilingual Education* (Transaction Publishers, 1995).

2. Rosalie Pedalino Porter, *American Immigrant: My Life in Three Languages* (New York: iUniverse, 2009), 425.

3. Ibid.

4. Rosalie Pedalino Porter, e-mail to the author, August 6, 2012.

5. Porter, *American Immigrant*, citing the annual October Individual Schools Reports and the Transitional Bilingual Education Report.

6. Christine H. Rossell and Keith Baker, *Bilingual Education in Massachusetts: The Emperor has no Clothes* (Boston: Pioneer Institute for Public Policy Research, 1996), 1.

7. Ibid., 160.

8. "Language Barrier: Minorities Need Assimilation, Not Segregation," *Worcester Telegram & Gazette,* April 24, 1996, http://www.onenation.org/1996/042496.html.

9. Rossell and Baker, *Bilingual Education in Massachusetts*, 160.

10. "A Wise Vote in Any Language," *Boston Globe*, April 13, 1995, http://www.onenation.org/1995/041395.html.

11. Rossell and Baker, *Bilingual Education in Massachusetts*, 1.

12. Ibid., 202–203.

13. Muriel Cohen, "Teach in English, Urges New Book on Bilingual Education," *Boston Globe*, May 19, 1996, http://www.onenation.org/1996/051996.html.

14. Ibid.

15. Ibid.

16. Jordana Hart, "Bilingual Classes Expected to Be Hot Issue Here," *Boston Globe*, June 4, 1998, http://www.onenation.org/0698/060498z.html.

17. Ibid.

18. Carol McDonald, "Calif. Law Fuels Mass. Debate on Fate of Bilingual Education," *Worcester Telegram & Gazette*, August 24, 1998, http://www.onenation.org/0898/082498.html.

19. Jordana Hart, "Bilingual Students Excused from Test," *Boston Globe*, November 1, 1998, http://www.onenation.org/1198/110198a.html.

20. Rebecca Duran, "Massachusetts Legislators Debate Fate of Bilingual Education System," *Boston University Daily Free Press*, January 12, 2000, http://www.onenation.org/0001/011200.html.

21. Guy W. Glodis, "Current Bilingual Education Fails," *Worcester Telegram & Gazette*, January 27, 2000, http://www.onenation.org/opinion/current-bilingual-education-fails/.

22. Jordana Hart, "Protesters Assail Filing of Bill to End State Bilingual Education," *Boston Globe*, January 12, 2000, http://www.onenation.org/0001/011200b.html.

23. Ibid.

24. Ibid.

25. Martin Finucane, "Bilingual Ed Proposal Brings Swift Criticism," Associated Press, January 11, 2000, http://www.onenation.org/0001/011100b.html.

26. Shaun Sutner, "Bilingual Reform Facing Battle," *Worcester Telegram & Gazette*, August 1, 2001, http://www.onenation.org/0108/080101c.htm.

27. Ibid.

28. Ibid.

29. Ibid.

30. Ibid.

31. Izzy Lyman, "English for the Children was David v. Goliath Victory," MassNews.com, April 15, 2003, http://www.massnews.com/2003_Editions/4_April/041503_mn_english_for_the_children.html.

32. Scott S. Greenberger, "Bilingual Ed Loses Favor with Some Educators," *Boston Globe*, August 5, 2001, http://www.puertorico-herald.org/issues/2001/vol5n33/BilingEd-en.html.

33. Porter, *American Immigrant*, 427.

34. Ibid.

35. "Question 2: Law Proposed by Initiative Petition, English Language Instruction in Public Schools," *The Official Massachusetts information for Voters, The 2002 Ballot Questions* (published by William Francis Galvin, Secretary of the Commonwealth), 6, https://www.sec.state.ma.us/ele/elepdf/ifv02.pdf.

36. "Bilingual Balderdash," *Wall Street Journal*, October 11, 2002, http://online.wsj.com/article/0,,SB103430393280794076.djm,00.html.

37. Richard Nangle, "Bilingual Ed Produces Stark Divide," *Worcester Telegram & Gazette*, October 6, 2002. Can be accessed through the Telegram.com Newsbank Online Archives at http://www.telegram.com/archives.

38. Clive McFarlane, "Swift OKs Bilingual Ed Reform Bill," *Worcester Telegram & Gazette*, August 7, 2002. Can be accessed at Telegram.com Newsbank Online Archives at http://www.telegram.com/archives.

39. Samuel L. Blumenfeld, "Massachusetts Embraces English," *WorldNet Daily*, November 8, 2002, http://www.freerepublic.com/focus/news/784961/posts.

40. "Bilingual Balderdash."

41. Porter, *American Immigrant*, 428–29.

42. Ron Unz, "Liberal Massachusetts and Conservative Colorado," *Writings and Perspectives*, November 8, 2002, http://ronunz.org/2002/11/08/liberal-massachusetts-and-conservative-colorado.

43. Sandra Stotsky, *An Empty Curriculum* (Latham, MD: Rowman & Littlefield, 2015), ix–x.

44. Ibid., 55.

45. Ibid., 56–57.

46. Ibid., 57.

47. World-Class Instructional Design and Assessment Consortium, "ACCESS for ELLs 2.0 Accessibility and Accommodations *Descriptions*," Massachusetts Department of Elementary and Secondary Education, August 10, 2015, 7, https://www.wida.us/assessment/WIDA_AccessAccDescriptions.pdf.

48. Massachusetts Department of Elementary and Secondary Education, "2007 NAEP Tests: Summary of Results for Massachusetts," 2007, 20–22, http://www.doe.mass.edu/mcas/natl-intl/naep/results/07read_math.pdf.

49. Board of Elementary and Secondary Education Proficiency Gap Task Force, "A Roadmap to Closing the Proficiency Gap," April 2010, 13, http://archives.lib.state.ma.us/bitstream/handle/2452/127648/ocn806088204.pdf?sequence=1.

50. Jaclyn Zubrzycki, "Feds Prompt Massachusetts to Require ELL Training," *Education Week*, Vol. 31, Issue 05, September 28, 2011.

51. Rachel Slama, Erin Haynes, Lynne Sacks, Dong Hoon Lee, and Diane August, *Profiles and Progress: A Report for the Massachusetts Department of Elementary and Secondary Education* (Washington, DC: American Institutes for Research, 2015), http://www.doe.mass.edu/research/reports/2015/10MA-ELLStudyReport.pdf.

52. "ED Data Express: Data about Elementary and Secondary Schools in the U.S.," US Department of Education, ED.gov, https://eddataexpress.ed.gov/state-tables-main.cfm. No comparison was made between the MA monitored former limited English proficient (MFLEP) students and "all students" because the American Institutes For Research (AIR) data of comparisons at the school level was available and more relevant. Moreover, the greater difficulty of the MCAS compared to the other state tests made a true comparison impossible.

53. Stotsky, *An Empty Curriculum*, xiii.

54. Colin A. Young, "Michigan Senate Panel Turns to Old Mass. MCAS Standards," State House News Service, May 3, 2016.

Index

About the Author

Johanna J. Haver has been a member of the Maricopa County Community College District Board since January 2015 and presently holds the office of board secretary. She has thirty-two years of teaching experience in the areas of German, Latin, reading, English, and English as a second language in K–12 schools and at the university level. She taught English as a visiting teacher at a *Gymnasium* for one year in Essen-Steele, Germany, and as a Phoenix Sister City teacher at a high school for two years in Himeji, Japan.

Since 1996 she has written several articles, mostly on education, for the *Arizona Republic*, the *East Valley Tribune*, and the *San Francisco Daily Journal*. She is the author of two previous books: *Structured English Immersion* (2003) and *English for the Children* (2013).

Presently, she lives in Phoenix, Arizona, with her husband Lloyd Engel. She visits her daughter, son-in-law, and two grandsons frequently in Palo Alto, California.

www.ingramcontent.com/pod-product-compliance
Lightning Source LLC
Chambersburg PA
CBHW062032270326
41929CB00014B/2408